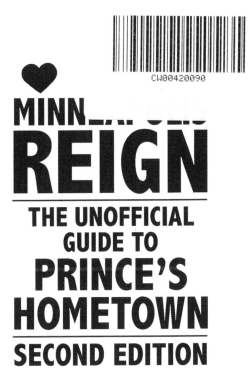

MINNEAPOLIS
REIGN

THE UNOFFICIAL GUIDE TO
PRINCE'S
HOMETOWN

SECOND EDITION

SECOND EDITION

Published in paperback in 2018 by Sixth Element Publishing
on behalf of Stuart Willoughby

Sixth Element Publishing
Arthur Robinson House
13-14 The Green
Billingham TS23 1EU
Tel: 01642 360253
www.6epublishing.net

© Stuart Willoughby 2018

ISBN 978-1-912218-40-0

British Library Cataloguing in Publication Data. A catalogue record for this book is
available from the British Library.

Printed in Great Britain.

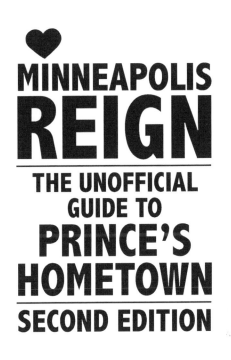

MINNEAPOLIS
REIGN

THE UNOFFICIAL GUIDE TO
PRINCE'S
HOMETOWN

SECOND EDITION

STUART WILLOUGHBY

PRAISE FOR MINNEAPOLIS REIGN

"Far more than a travelogue or adoring fan
paean, the author writes with journalistic acuity.
He has created a book that is respectful, thorough,
educational, and entertaining. Commendable."

Alex Hahn, author of Possessed: The Rise and Fall of Prince

"(Minneapolis Reign) needs to be read to be believed.
Boasts an attention to detail that will enable fans to
follow his steps to even the hardest-to-find locations.
For the fan, the fam, or the just plain curious,
the book more than makes good on its promise."

*Jason Draper, author of Prince: Life & Times and
Prince: Chaos, Disorder & Revolution*

"A heartfelt narrative, and incredibly poignant.
Stuart is such a good-natured and enthusiastic guide
you can bet I'll be tracing some of his travels myself."

Laura Tiebert, author of The Rise of Prince 1958-1988

"An amazing read. This is clearly the work of a man
dealing with dual emotions of sorrow and excitement.
A deep and impressive knowledge. Formidable."

Michael Byars, KCUR-FM, Kansas City, USA

"Heartbreak, joy, laughter, and tears, perfectly captured.
This may prove to be one of the most important
Prince books I have ever read. Thank you."

Nigel Hart, UK

"Prince is smiling down on you, Stuart."

Tami Foster, USA

"The excitement, the sorrow, the thrill and the heartache are all evident. Stuart is at once informative, then grief-stricken, funny, then philosophical. A wonderful read."
Katie Jones, UK

"A book for anyone who loves music. The attention to detail is astounding. I learned a lot about an artist I knew very little of. A great credit to the way the story is told."
Chris Bailey, UK

"The ultimate guide for any Prince fan, and the ultimate tribute to the man, the icon, the superstar."
Carolyn Chester, UK

"Beautifully observed, deeply researched, and very moving. A definitive guide for anyone wanting to visit Minneapolis."
Philip Clarkson, UK

"A VIP pass to the world of Prince. Best of all, it's written from the perspective of one of us… a fan."
Gill Fullick, UK

"A must-have for all who love and miss Prince Rogers Nelson."
Karen Surmiak, USA

"You'll laugh and you'll cry. Thank you, Stuart, for this remarkable story."
Jeannine Gila, USA

ACKNOWLEDGEMENTS

This book is dedicated 2 my wife and children.
Thank U 4 everything.

2 Jonathan Tait, Ben Thompson and Mark Flanagan.
Thank U 4 the Trip.

Xtra Thanx 2 Jonathan. Your memory has proved invaluable.

And finally, 2 Prince Rogers Nelson.
Thank U 4 the Songs.

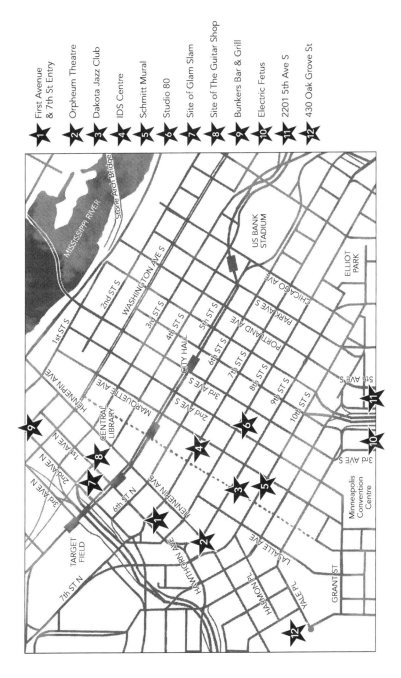

1. First Avenue & 7th St Entry
2. Orpheum Theatre
3. Dakota Jazz Club
4. IDS Centre
5. Schmitt Mural
6. Studio 80
7. Site of Glam Slam
8. Site of The Guitar Shop
9. Bunkers Bar & Grill
10. Electric Fetus
11. 2201 5th Ave S
12. 430 Oak Grove St

Family: *noun*
1. A group consisting of two parents and their children living together as a unit.
2. A group of people united by certain convictions or a common affiliation.
3. A group of related things.

Prince didn't call us fans. He called us 'family' or *'fam'* for short. To honour him – and to honour his *fam* – I will use this term throughout this recollection.

"I know that people who don't care about music will think it ridiculous – and in many ways it probably is – but tonight, I am absolutely heartbroken. I've never cried over the death of a celebrity before today, but the funny little man I have looked up to and idolised since I was a boy of twelve years old is gone. And I can't comprehend it. With the exception of my father, Prince Rogers Nelson has probably influenced my life more than anyone else, and he was – and always will be – my absolute musical hero. He was everything I wanted to be when I was growing up, effortlessly cool, worshipped by girls, and for my money, the most outrageously talented musician of an age. Those of you who have known me since I was a little kid with a massive obsession will know just how much he means to me. Today, I feel like a part of what made me who I am has died with him. He was my Lennon. My Elvis. My Bowie. Thanks for your messages, everyone. They're much appreciated."

Stu
April 21st 2016

TUESDAY

As the plane descended through the clouds, I took a deep breath. After twelve hours in the air, I was almost there. It was within touching distance. Strangely, I felt like I already knew this city. It was like I'd always known it.

Minneapolis was the city of his birth. It was the city in which he had lived. It was the city in which he had worked. Now, it was the city in which he had died. In three days, it would be the first anniversary of that seismic event. I was about to immerse myself in his world completely and experience places that were a real part of his life. Places that I had only read about in books and magazines, or seen on television. Nonetheless, I felt like I knew this city, for its favourite son had called to me since I was a boy.

Uptown. First Avenue. Lake Minnetonka. Paisley Park.

For as long as I could remember, these places had seemed as familiar to me as my own little town, back home in the North East of England.

When I was growing up, I lived in a house where music was played constantly. The stereo was on more than the television when I was a kid. My father, Lawrence, had a huge record collection of classic rock and folk albums from the '60s and '70s, and he had always been into audio equipment. My uncle was the boss of a hi-fi store, so Dad was forever upgrading to the latest gear. My love of good quality sound systems is inherited from them both. Whenever neighbourhood kids would come to my

1

house and listen to records, they would always complain that their parents' hi-fi didn't sound like ours. For almost the first decade of my life, I listened to nothing but my dad's records. We'd sit and play them, and I'd scrutinise the sleeves, reading the liner notes and asking many questions, while Dad would regale me with tales of all the bands he had seen. My own record collection now includes dozens of albums he used to play to me. A few of them are actually the very same copies.

I'd dabbled with a bit of punk music when I was just nine years old. That seems very young, I know, but my interest was piqued by the family babysitter, Frankie. He was a punk and had gotten into Adam and the Ants in a big way, and it just rubbed off on me, I guess. In February 1980 – for my ninth birthday – I bought Adam's first LP *Dirk Wears White Sox*, which had been released a few months earlier. My mother, Georgina, wasn't impressed with some of the lyrics and thought the record inappropriate for me, but Dad said it was okay and I played it pretty much non-stop for the rest of that year. When Adam's breakthrough album *Kings of the Wild Frontier* came out in the winter of 1980, I'd been a fan for months already thanks to Frankie. My friends all bought *Kings*, but none of them were aware that there had been an album before it. When I played it to them, they thought it was very strange as it sounded nothing like the album that the band had just released in their bid for pop stardom. In 1981, Adam and the Ants released *Prince Charming*, which sounded even more radio-friendly. Around this time, I began listening to the music charts. I'd still never heard electronic dance music.

One day, a friend invited me over to his house after school. As we sat in the living room, his older brother – who I'd guess must have been eighteen or so – was playing a record on a little turntable in the next room. I began listening to the music, and I slowly lost interest in whatever movie my friend and I had been watching on TV. I wandered into the other room and asked his brother who the record was by. As I recall it now, he didn't really know that much about it. I expect he may have just borrowed it from a friend. He handed me the purple sleeve.

A pair of piercing brown eyes – belonging to what appeared to be a pink and white striped creature of some kind – stared at me amongst the collages that made up the lettering on the front cover. I stared at it for a few minutes, picking out all the different things I could see. Some of it looked like it had been drawn with a felt tip pen. There was a little ladder. And a pair of pinstripe pants. The 'c' was a mouth full of crooked teeth turned on its side. And hang on, that strange-looking number one in the title; is that what I think it is? Wow. Yes, it's *one of those alright*. I was so shocked that I almost didn't notice the tiny backward lettering right in the centre of the sleeve: 'And The Revolution'. I didn't know who or what The Revolution was. Little did I know it then, but within a year, I would be obsessed with them. I sat down and we listened to this incredibly hypnotic music that was like nothing I'd ever heard before. Pulling the inner bag out of the record sleeve, I studied the photo on one side of it. It showed a naked black guy in a bedroom that was illuminated in red and yellow neon. He was sprawled on the bed, and a thin blue satin sheet was just barely covering him. He was looking right at me. Behind him – through the window – a crescent moon hung in the jet black sky, and an unearthly laser beam fired into the bedroom from outside, causing a plume of smoke that billowed around the room as it hit the wall opposite. On the floor was a large neon love heart. This picture – and the sounds I was hearing – completely altered the trajectory of my music taste in a heartbeat. It was summer 1983. The record was *1999*, and I was twelve years old.

I put my tray table in the upright position, fastened the belt across my lap, and closed my eyes. Listening to *1999* through my earphones, I pictured Paisley Park in my mind. It was an entire industry in one huge gleaming white complex on the outskirts of Minneapolis that he had built in a strange sounding place called Chanhassen. Paisley Park housed the very studios where the wonderful songs that had provided the background music for most of my life experiences were recorded. Of course, it wasn't just a workplace. It was also his home. And I'd be there in just a few hours. I made a note to buy my wife – who had stayed at home with the kids – a nice gift to say thank you for allowing me to do this crazy thing.

In 2006, she and I had travelled across America from New York to California. We saw dozens of landmarks on our journey, and at every one I had that strange otherworldly feeling you get when you're confronted with a place – particularly in the United States when you're from Britain, I find – that has only previously existed in one's subconscious and has, more often than not, usually been gleaned from popular culture.

I'd felt it at Ground Zero. I'd felt it on Alcatraz. And I'd felt it at the Grand Canyon. When you're experiencing those places for real, I've often found that you're still perfectly capable of looking at your surroundings objectively and can be totally aware that people who spend their lives there find it completely normal – or perhaps even mundane – as they go about their ordinary business around you. Yet you still can't help being overawed by your experience and can sometimes even feel a little foolish. Or maybe that's just me.

I remember being on the Observation Deck of the Empire State Building once, and speaking to a guy who worked in the gift store that is a nausea-inducing twelve hundred feet from the ground. It turned out – much to my surprise – that he was from my town back in England. I told him excitedly that he was unbelievably lucky to work in such an amazing location.

He simply shrugged and said, "It's just a job."

I laughed, but I actually felt a little embarrassed. The second I left the store though, I was back in full-on awestruck tourist mode.

I thought about that familiar sensation as I contemplated what lay ahead in the coming days. I knew I'd be experiencing it again soon. I'd played this scenario out in my mind dozens of times over the years. Of course, I never imagined in a million years that I would be doing it, but what had happened had happened, and here I was. It suddenly seemed a little too real. My incredible adventure in Minneapolis was about to begin. I had no way of knowing it at the time, but the coming days would surpass my wildest dreams. Right then though, I was apprehensive about the whole thing, and I didn't know how I was going to cope emotionally with seeing the place Prince had called home. It was all I could do to stop myself from crying. When I was booking the trip in the fall of 2016, like many *fam*, I was still hurting badly over the loss I had felt since April, and I hoped that coming to Minnesota would in some small way help to heal that pain and somehow make his passing seem more bearable.

The plane circled and we began the final approach to Minneapolis-Saint Paul Airport, and I thought back to that terrible day in early 2016, and how I had felt. As the news had broken, I had immediately received dozens of messages and calls from friends and colleagues who knew how much he meant to me while I was growing up. When I heard the news of his passing, it hit me so hard. Such was the intensity of my pain, in fact, that even I was surprised at how distraught I was. I shut myself away in my room for a few days while I tried to process my sorrow at losing the man who, with the exception of my father, had meant more to me than any other, and yet was someone I'd never actually met. I have to say that my wife and children were my solace at this time. I'd never cried at the death of a celebrity before – much less someone I didn't know in person – and this sudden outpouring of my emotions was completely alien to me. Looking back now, I think it particularly upset my wife to see me like that. She has always been my rock, and I hated her seeing me cry. My genuine heartache at the loss of a rock musician on the other side of the Atlantic surprised us both.

After a few days I managed to pull myself around a little and began talking about what had happened. The rumour mill was in overdrive as the papers whipped themselves into a frenzy speculating on the cause of Prince's passing, and I pored over them trying to make some sense of it all. The official cause of his demise took six weeks to deliver, and when it arrived it caused a whole new series of heartaches for his *fam*. Had Prince secretly been in a lot of pain? Had he been alone when he died? In a matter of a few hours, I would be at Paisley Park where this tragedy that had shocked the world had actually taken place. As I thought about that, I really couldn't comprehend it.

I wasn't travelling to Minneapolis alone. When I'd decided to do this, I'd put a call out on social media inviting anyone who wanted to embark on this four thousand mile voyage with me to get in touch.

Jonathan – a young man who used to work with me – asked if he could come. Jonathan was twenty. He was a few years younger than my eldest daughter, but he seemed a lot older. His family lived near me in a small town called Billingham, and his mother Andrea – who I'd known for several years – was a champion dancer in her youth. Jonathan's love of music was inherited from her. He was studying English at the University of York and was writing his final dissertation on Prince, I believe. He'd been a *fam* for six or seven years now. When Prince passed, Jonathan got a tattoo to commemorate his life. He reminded me of myself when I was younger. Most people who know both of us say the same thing. Once the trip was agreed, we put together an itinerary of Prince-related locations to visit. The list was pretty comprehensive.

A little later, Jonathan asked if his friend Ben – who he'd known since school – could accompany us. Ben was the same age as Jonathan, and was currently studying Music Production at Leeds Beckett University. Ben had been a Prince nut since he was a little kid. He actually looked uncannily like a young Mr Rogers Nelson. I'd remarked on it the very first time I met him. Ben's parents had paid for him to come to Minneapolis as a surprise Christmas present. Jonathan was in on it, and somehow they managed to keep it a secret until the big day. Ben's knowledge of Prince's music was first rate.

As we touched down on the runway, thoughts of Prince's passing – and the media frenzy it had created – tumbled through my mind. I was quickly brought back to the present by a friendly-looking elderly man sitting to my left.

"You guys here for business or pleasure?" he asked.

"Well, I'm not really sure," I replied, then, "We're just here for Prince." I knew as soon as I said it that it would sound a little crazy, but I didn't really care. At that moment, I honestly didn't know whether this trip was for business or pleasure either. All I knew for sure was that it was something I felt completely compelled to do. It felt 100% necessary for me to be here.

"Ah, I see," said the old guy, as if no further explanation was needed. He proceeded to tell us about his business – which was something to do with motorcycles as I recall – but I wasn't really paying much attention and his conversation didn't sink in. I looked outside and it looked like we could be in any airport in the world. It wasn't just any airport though. It was Prince's airport. I'd heard that Minneapolis was cold this time of year. It certainly looked it.

We departed the plane and I walked through the concourse alongside the huge windows on my right looking out over the airfield. It was overcast and looked like there might be a thunderstorm coming. Spots of rain started to appear on the glass. I began thinking about the car I had hired and hoped I would be okay on the roads here. I'd not driven in America before, so I was a little concerned. To the left of us was the baggage carousel. The airport looked old-fashioned. I remember thinking that the carpet looked like it might have been there since the '70s.

We joined the queue for US Customs and I looked around. There were a few people wearing purple, and I spotted Prince's Love Symbol – the peculiar and unpronounceable glyph he went by the name of – dotted around on a couple of bags and cases. One of the flight attendants had told us on the plane that there was a party of Prince *fam* onboard who were having a high old time all the way across the Atlantic. It made me happy to know that we weren't the only ones doing this, even though I knew I probably wouldn't be meeting them.

You should know that about me. I'm kind of a solitary

guy really. I'm popular and I have lots of friends and a loving family, but on the rare occasions that I get the opportunity to be alone I'm quite happy in my own company, and this trip wasn't intended as an opportunity to meet like-minded people if I'm being honest. But don't get me wrong, I enjoy meeting people. And I like people who love things passionately. I totally understand what it's like to worship someone famous too. I get it completely.

My friend Shane is obsessed with the British rock band, Status Quo. I've been to his house. It's like a shrine to them. He collects not only their music, but memorabilia too. My own Prince-related collection is huge – much to my wife's chagrin – so I know what it's like to have that all-consuming dedication. I also knew exactly how others who loved him felt about Prince. I'd met lots of them at his shows. I was certain too that they would know how much he meant to me, so I didn't feel the need to share the impact Prince had had on my life on this trip. I'd actually said as much to Jonathan and Ben before we'd left home, saying, "You need to understand that I'm doing this for me. You're coming along for the ride and it'll be amazing so you'd better hang on tight, but this is for *me*."

I got stuck for a moment at the US Border Control desk as the guy's computer broke down as it took my photo, and while we waited for it to reboot, he slipped out of his stern official persona and we chatted for a minute or two. He asked me why I was in Minneapolis.

"Prince," I said, like it was a perfectly reasonable response.

"Okay," he laughed.

I remarked that it had been a year since Prince's passing.

"Wow," said the Border Control officer. "That came around quick."

He mentioned that he had collected Prince LPs when he was younger, and I told him that I worked in music retail with a particular focus on vinyl records.

"I hear they're coming back," he said.

"They are indeed," I replied, and he ushered me on my way with a "Good day, Sir."

I met up with Jonathan and Ben who had been waiting for me. We found a restroom, freshened up, and headed for the car rental desk.

It was a short shuttle journey and an escalator ride or two away, and after a few minutes we approached the desk. A young lady took my details, welcomed us to the United States, and asked if I'd driven in America before. I told her it was my first time, and she flashed a brilliant smile and said I'd be okay. I joked that I wasn't as sure as I hadn't driven an automatic for twenty-five years, and she replied that I'd be used to it in no time.

"That's easy for you to say," I laughed. "The steering wheel is on the wrong side of the car for me, and I'm also on the opposite side of the road than I'm used to."

The girl chuckled, saying, "Oh my. You'd better get used to it real quick then, Sir!"

I made a joke about hoping the car would be coming back in one piece and she said, "Don't worry. It's fine. You've got our premium *'get out of jail'* insurance package, Mr Willoughby. You could literally do anything to it and walk away a free man."

I smiled and she handed me my documents. I thanked her for her help and we were shown to the parking lot.

A young guy in a suit that was clearly too big for him came over to me and explained that our car was on its way, so we waited patiently for it to arrive. After five minutes he apologised and went to the desk to find out where our car was. We waited for a further five minutes before he came back and apologised again. Nearby was a gleaming black Audi with the door open. The car looked brand new. He motioned us towards it.

"Would this be okay, Sir?" he enquired. "It's the next model up from the one you ordered but I'm not sure we have a car ready for you."

I looked at the car. I'd ordered a standard model. This was definitely not a standard model.

"Are you sure?" I said. "This one looks expensive."

He left us for a moment and went to the desk. After a beat, he came back and handed me the keys, saying, "It's fine, Sir. You can take this one."

He gave me the GPS unit which I handed to Jonathan, and we sat in the car while he quickly went through the controls.

The car smelled of new leather upholstery. I glanced at the milometer. The car had done just twelve hundred miles. It was literally only a few weeks old. I felt even more nervous for seeing that, and momentarily had a vision of me totalling a brand new forty-thousand dollar automobile. I put all such thoughts out of my mind and we were good to go.

I took a deep breath, looked outside, saw that it was starting to get dark, and said, "Hold on to your hats, guys."

And with that, we were off.

We slowly followed the direction signs and left the airport, and as I quickly familiarised myself with the car, we joined the freeway heading southwest towards Chanhassen. It was a twenty-mile drive to the hotel, and I was pleased it wasn't too far because the sky was growing darker by the minute. Being on the opposite side of the road than I was used to back home felt stranger than the occasions when I had driven in continental Europe – where people also drive on the right – and I put it down to the car being left hand drive, whereas my own car isn't. I was particularly wary of other vehicles joining traffic from the right and undertaking being the norm, but after ten minutes or so I began to feel a little more comfortable. So comfortable in fact, that we even had the radio on for a while. Jonathan – who is au fait with technology – quickly set the GPS with our hotel address and we continued onward into the outskirts of Minneapolis.

We were staying at the Country Inn and Suites by Carlson at 591 West 78th Street in Chanhassen, which was just a short five-minute drive from Paisley Park. We decided that instead of going straight there, we would take a quick detour to Audubon Road – where Prince's complex is located – and I headed in that direction.

It was huge. As we drove along Arboretum Boulevard in Chanhassen, we chattered excitedly about Paisley Park, when suddenly – almost out of nowhere in the darkness – it hoved into view on the left side of the road. It was bathed in a soft purple glow. *Of course it was.* The blue-green pyramidal roof-lights on top of the building were clearly visible, and for the first time on this trip my breath was truly taken away. We didn't speak. Our stunned silence a result of what we were looking at.

I used to work in commercial building design. Unusual or striking architecture always fascinates me, and I've seen – and even worked on – some famous buildings, but this was something else entirely. I couldn't quite comprehend the fact that I was looking at Prince's home. I was four thousand miles from my little house back in England, and for a few minutes my brain was unable to process the fact that I was sitting in a car outside the very building where the incredible music I have loved from the age of twelve was created, and it was absolutely, resolutely, and darn-tootin'-ly spectacular.

The 65,000 square foot structure was of a quintessentially '80s design, with huge ice-white panels covering the entire place, but at the same time it still looked super-futuristic a full three decades after its completion.

From the freeway, I took a left onto Audubon Road and we found that we were on what can only be described as an *industrial park*. I'd obviously seen footage and photos of Paisley Park – and I was aware that it was located just off a busy main road – but I was surprised to find that it was surrounded by many businesses and looked remarkably like an *industrial estate* – as they are known in the UK – that is only a few minutes from my very own home. We also discovered that the complex was flanked on one side by a children's Day Care centre, and a Kindergarten on the other.

I turned the car around on a little dead-end street called McGlynn Drive opposite the gates to Paisley Park, and we sat there for a few minutes just looking at the towering white monolith standing before us. Looking back now, I remember that I was at once overwhelmed yet strangely calm and – to my absolute surprise – I did not cry. I had fully expected to shed tears when I saw Prince's home for the first time, but as I sat there looking across the street at Paisley Park I think I was too taken aback by the fact that I was really there to be upset. In fact, I was more excited than anything. Our adventure had truly started. I recall looking at Jonathan and Ben's faces and it was clear to see that they were as astonished as I was.

We took a few photos and began to point out interesting things about the building and its grounds to each other, including the property number – 7801 – high up on the side wall, and I cracked a funny about the possibility of the mailman not knowing the address. By then it was as dark as night and much as we would have liked to sit and revel in the view before us, we decided to go to our hotel.

Chanhassen is a beautiful suburb on the outskirts of Minneapolis. It covers an area of twenty-two square miles, and has a population of just over twenty thousand. In the past, it has won awards for being amongst the best places to live in America. It's not difficult to see why. The streets are immaculately kept, and the city places importance on parks and open spaces. There are miles of trails to explore, and the city boasts several beautiful beaches.

Homes in Chanhassen are a mix of upmarket apartment buildings and gorgeous colonial-style weatherboard houses. Some of them are huge and offer stunning views from prime locations along the shorelines of the numerous lakes that pepper the area. I'd kill to live there. Chanhassen has the same feel to it as those UK holiday village-type destinations us Brits are familiar with, albeit one with houses on a much grander scale. Our hotel was located right in the middle of the city, and we found it with ease. It was surrounded by local eateries and stores.

As we pulled into the Country Inn and Suites parking lot, a neon sign nearby flashed the legend 'Welcome Prince *Fam*'. I smiled and pointed it out to my companions and for a moment we watched as the message changed to 'Purple Reign 1958-2016'. We grabbed our bags and headed inside.

The young woman on the front desk informed me that I was in room number 355. Jonathan was next door in 356, and Ben was across the corridor in 360. I laughed to myself and wished I'd been allocated room '319'; the title of a Prince tune from 1995's *The Gold Experience* album. Arriving at our final destination after a very long day of travelling suddenly made me feel very weary and we decided to freshen up before venturing out for food. The receptionist informed us that there were restaurants and bars all around the hotel, and after walking down the wrong corridor – which I seem to do in every hotel I ever stay in – we took the elevator to our floor and agreed to meet in the lobby in thirty minutes.

Inside my room, I threw my case on the couch and made a call to my wife to let her know that I had arrived safely. It was 7.30pm in Chanhassen, but realising that it was 1.30am back home I figured that she'd be asleep, so I didn't expect her to answer and I just intended to leave a message. To my astonishment, she picked up almost immediately and said sleepily, "Hi."

I apologised for waking her and I let her know that I was in the hotel and that I hadn't yet crashed the car. She laughed. I was only half-joking. I quickly told her about my day and I asked after the kids and then I told her to get some sleep. She hung up and I headed out for dinner with Jonathan and Ben.

We walked outside and it was quiet. There was a chill in the air but the sky was clear and black. We turned right – without crossing the street – and walked along the buildings next door to the hotel. At the end of the block was the famous Chanhassen Dinner Theater, which is reputed to be the largest professional dinner theatre in the US. It has enough seating for almost a thousand patrons. Before we reached that though, we passed the Christian Science Reading Room and spotted a bar a few doors down called Chuck Wagon Charlie's Smokehouse and Saloon, which was located at 545 West 78th Street.

The place looked deserted and I tried the door. It was open. We went inside and save for the barkeeper there was only one other customer in the place. He was sitting at the bar and he was very drunk. He acknowledged us with a grunt and we sat at a table. The barkeep – a sporty good-looking guy – welcomed us and he was taken aback slightly when I spoke and he realised we were British. He introduced himself as Shane, and he asked us why we were in town.

After explaining – much to his astonishment – that we were Prince *fam* who had travelled to Chanhassen to see Paisley Park, he fixed us some drinks and sat with us to chat. He told us that his eight-year old niece once spoke to Prince in a local store. Shane laughed as he said that he didn't even attempt to get near our man – who was naturally flanked by his security – but reported that Prince happily spoke to his niece before leaving the store.

We ordered food and while we waited for it to arrive, the inebriated guy ambled past us unsteadily and grunted something that was indecipherable, before leaving. As the food was being prepared we could hear lots of shouting coming from the kitchen. Shane shouted back at whoever was in there and then looked at us while shrugging his shoulders and grinning.

Shane sat with us while we ate and he drew up a small list of local attractions we might like to check out while we were in town.

"If you guys can drag yourselves away from all the Prince stuff, that is," he joked.

I took the list and thanked him but I had a feeling we wouldn't be getting to many – if any – of them. The food was delicious, by the way. I'm not really a red meat eater so I ordered the 'Yardbird', a chicken burger tossed with onions, shredded cheddar, mustard, and served with the most amazing fries and coleslaw. In traditional American style, my plate was piled high but I was hungry and managed to finish almost all of it. Jonathan chose something similarly gargantuan – the 'Smokestack', I think – that was chock-full of meat, while Ben, who weighs about half what I do, opted for something a bit smaller, possibly macaroni cheese with burnt ends. By the way, Jonathan had an unbelievable appetite and could easily be a competitive eater. I'm not kidding. He wolfed his food down within what seemed like mere seconds and didn't even break a sweat. He laughed and said, "I don't like food if it isn't hot!" I cursed his youthful metabolism and wished I could eat whatever I wanted without feeling guilty about it for a day or two.

Shane topped up our drinks and we chatted some more after we had eaten, before we bid him goodnight saying that we'd be back.

We retired to our rooms and I flopped onto the bed, tired but ecstatic to be there. I decided to send a quick message to my friend Michael who lived in Kansas City. Michael was an announcer on the NPR station KCUR-FM, and we had been friends for several years. He once travelled to my town in the UK, but I was on vacation at the time so we'd never actually met in person. We weren't meeting up on this trip either sadly, as my visit coincided with the station's busiest week of the year and Michael couldn't get the time off work. I feel a strong bond with him though, and we often send each other gifts and speak regularly. Although we live thousands of miles apart, I feel like he is a close friend and I would hope that he thinks the same too.

I sent Michael one word: "Minneapolis".

He responded almost immediately saying, "Welcome to America!" before jokily telling me that, "We aren't all lunatics, I promise."

I ran through my first few hours in his country and we yakked about nothing much at all really. He offered me some great driving advice, and asked about the hotel, the food, and my itinerary for the next day. He told me that, "Minnesota is good country." So far, I had every reason to believe him and I felt a surge of excitement about the days ahead. Michael signed off by asking me to keep him up to date with my activities.

After a while, I showered and tried to sleep. Unfortunately, my body clock was out of whack and – at around midnight – I suddenly realised that I'd been awake for over twenty-four hours. I opened the curtains and looked out over the Chanhassen rooftops and the quiet street outside. I watched the traffic lights blinking and thought back to the moment we had sat in the car across the street from Paisley Park. Unbelievably, I was now in Prince's town. I smiled and then suddenly felt a tinge of sadness and my eyes began to water. I can't explain why. Looking back now, I think perhaps that this was the moment the realisation of what I was doing – and why I was here – finally hit me. I dried my eyes and got into bed. I set my alarm for my usual rising time of 6.00am, and then promptly woke up after approximately two hours sleep.

WEDNESDAY

I met Jonathan and Ben for breakfast at 7.00am the next morning, and we talked about the day ahead. We had booked a tour of First Avenue and 7th St Entry, the club where most of the action in the movie *Purple Rain* takes place. *Purple Rain* is a semi-autobiographical movie starring Prince that – along with the soundtrack album of the same name – catapulted him to superstardom in 1984. We were scheduled to begin the tour of First Avenue at 10.30am.

Over a breakfast of traditional American waffles, pancakes, and bacon and a European 'continental' style buffet, we looked over the list of places we intended to visit today, deciding to park the car in the city and then tackle the locations around First Avenue on foot, or by cab if needed.

After finishing our meal, we headed to the car and set off on the thirty-minute drive to Downtown Minneapolis. We travelled east along MN-5, before taking the exit onto Interstate 494E, followed by I-35W northward, and into the city.

Minneapolis is the largest city in the state of Minnesota, and it lies on both banks of the Mississippi River. It is adjoined to the city of Saint Paul which is the state capital. This gives rise to Minneapolis-Saint Paul being known as the 'Twin Cities'. Saint Paul is by far the older of the two cities and features an abundance of late-Victorian architecture. It has more of a bohemian feel to it with quaint neighbourhoods as opposed to the much younger Minneapolis, which has a more modern and cosmopolitan air with futuristic skyscrapers.

As we drove toward Minneapolis, the skyline was impressive – as most cities are – but it was not as huge as I had expected. Gleaming glass towers standing alongside red brick apartment blocks passed us by, and as the rush hour traffic stopped and started, we slowly made our way along the freeway as people all around us went about their ordinary day in the Twin Cities. It suddenly struck me that our day wasn't ordinary in the slightest, and I began to feel a long way from home. I often feel like that when I'm visiting a big city in another country. As we entered Downtown, we saw one of those city signs with the population number on it. 444,000. We marvelled at the fact that the city was smaller than we imagined, and is perhaps comparable in size to Leeds, a city approximately fifty miles from my town back in England.

We drove up to the third story in the first parking garage we came to, and comically congratulated each other on navigating the car thus far with no incidents to report. After asking a local how to pay for parking, we jumped in an elevator with him that took us to ground level.

Stepping outside onto South 7th Street, we headed northwest along it, and reassuringly the city of Minneapolis looked just like any city in the world. There was one difference though, and I spotted it immediately. The buildings around us were joined to each other by an elevated glass corridor two storeys up.

This system – called the 'Skyway' – was developed in 1962 and is a collection of interlinked enclosed footbridges that are climate controlled, connecting buildings in sixty-nine full city blocks covering an area of eleven miles. It's the biggest continuous walkway in the world, and it's a brilliant idea. Linking office towers, apartment buildings, hotels, banks, retail stores, government buildings, and even sports facilities, it allows Minneapolis residents to live, work, and shop Downtown without having to go outside, if they so desire.

We continued along South 7th and we spotted a street map on the left side of the street. We checked the location of the First Avenue club to confirm we were heading in the right direction, and used the opportunity to grab a few photos of ourselves at the map. Bemused locals walked past, busily going about their day and no doubt wondering why these three guys were not on their way to work but horsing around and taking pictures of each other. We continued past the Marriott Hotel on the right. Crossing Hennepin Avenue, we carried on walking onto North 7th Street, and suddenly the building on our left became recognisable. A small bar called The Depot marked the start of the First Avenue building.

First Avenue and 7th St Entry are two live music clubs housed in one iconic Minneapolis building on the corner of North 1st Avenue and North 7th Street. The building's brickwork is painted black, and the structure features five hundred and thirty one silver stars painted across its entire exterior commemorating past performers at this legendary American rock venue. With a combined capacity of approximately eighteen hundred, the art deco-styled building began life as a Greyhound bus station in 1937. When new, its state-of-the-art air conditioning, shower rooms, and chequered terrazzo floor were a wow with the locals. In 1968, the idea to turn the building into a music venue came about and – after a period of remodelling – the venue eventually opened its doors as The Depot on April 3, 1970 hosting British singer Joe Cocker as the very first act to play there. By a strange quirk of fate, I discovered recently that my mother – as a young woman – once spent a night dancing with Joe. The date you ask? February 8, 1970. Just two months earlier than the opening night of The Depot, and a year-and-a-day before my birth.

After further name changes – to Uncle Sam's and then just Sam's – on New Year's Eve 1981, the club became First Avenue and 7th St Entry. Playing his first show at Sam's on March 9, 1981 as part of the *Dirty Mind Tour*, and then again in October of that year, Prince's shows at the club went on to become the stuff of legend, and when it came to the production of *Purple Rain*, the choice of venue for the shooting of music scenes was never in question.

Anyone who has ever seen *Purple Rain* knows that First Avenue plays a major role in the movie. Prince performed at the club thirteen times throughout his career, often showcasing new material ahead of its official release. Prince's patronage revitalised the venue during the '80s, making it Minnesota's number one tourist attraction for several years, and it remained by far his favourite place to play. The club's owner during the filming of *Purple Rain*, Allan Fingerhut, credits Prince with keeping the club from financial ruin as it was losing money at the time, saying simply, "He saved the place."

Many of Prince's shows at First Avenue were organised with little notice and the club allowed him to perform whenever he wanted, which must have pleased Prince no end. The club became synonymous with its brightest star, and on that fateful day in April 2016 over ten thousand *fam* descended on First Avenue in an impromptu street party to pay their respects and say goodbye to Minneapolis' fallen son. This was followed by three all-night dance parties in the club which sold out instantly. Bobby Z – drummer with Prince's band The Revolution – referred to First Avenue as 'Ground Zero' in interviews after his friend's passing. Fittingly, the band chose the club as the very first place to play after their reunion in 2016, performing three sell-out shows. *Fam* flocked from around the world to see Prince's former bandmates pay an emotional homage to their late leader and mentor. Prince's star on the wall outside – which is the closest to the entrance – has been covered in gold leaf by an anonymous *fam*. First Avenue liked it and it has since become a permanent feature.

We arrived at First Avenue around 9.45am. We had forty-five minutes before our tour was due to begin, so we spent a little time outside taking photographs of each other and the club. Trying to get a decent snap of the entire building without catching local people or cars in the frame proved difficult and Jonathan, Ben, and I tried from all sorts of angles and positions until we were happy with the results. I stood across the street from the club's façade and Jonathan took a great photo of me from behind as I set off across the street facing toward the building.

We posed for photos outside the entrance foyer and then to the left of it underneath the little tatty and worn canvas canopy over the 7th St Entry doorway. The canopy looked like it had easily been there for over thirty years and we wondered for a moment if it was the original one from the *Purple Rain* days. We guessed that it probably would be, and proceeded to walk along the exterior looking at – and photographing – the silver stars that were dotted all over the brickwork, noting the names that had played at this iconic rock venue on each. I couldn't see a star with Joe Cocker's name on it. Suddenly, we came to Prince's gold star. Seeing it brought a sudden rush of emotion and I struggled to catch my breath for a moment. I pictured the scene from *Purple Rain* where Prince rides his motorcycle along the sidewalk outside the club. I was now standing on the very same spot. As I thought about this, I reached out and touched the star, just for a second. A single purple flower was pinned to the wall next to it with a thank you note from a British *fam* from Swindon.

I wandered across the street from First Avenue, and spoke to a lady from Chicago who was visiting Minneapolis and she was surprised to hear that I was British. She was wearing a Prince t-shirt and was booked on a later tour of First Avenue. After chatting for a few minutes, she wished us well on our trip and I headed back over to the entrance where a small crowd were gathered with a tour guide for the party that was just ahead of ours. We listened in for a few minutes while the guide pointed out the features of the building to the assembled visitors and they disappeared inside.

We still had thirty minutes to fill before our tour was due to start, so we decided to check out a couple of other spots on our itinerary first. They were close by so wouldn't take long to get to. As we headed to the first, we stumbled across a huge comic-book style piece of art completely by accident. It was painted on the side wall of the old National Camera Exchange at 930 Hennepin

Avenue. A brilliant pop-art piece by Greg Gossel, it features a pink Cadillac and a wide-eyed woman quoting a Prince lyric from 'Baby I'm A Star', a song from *Purple Rain*. We stopped to take photos of each other in front of it before moving on. I learned later that the piece was commissioned by American Express as part of a countrywide business initiative and was completed shortly before Prince's passing.

A minute later – and just two blocks from First Avenue – we were standing outside the beautiful Orpheum Theater at 910 Hennepin Avenue. Completed in 1921, this historic restored Beaux-Arts-style theatre – which once belonged to Bob Dylan – played host to Prince four times between 1980 and 2006. Interestingly, he only ever topped the bill there once. In 1989, he appeared onstage with Patti LaBelle. A decade later he was a guest at a Chaka Khan show. In his final performance at the venue in 2006, he appeared with Tamar Davis as part of her tour. His headlining 1980 show however, was a rescheduled date as part of his debut self-titled tour and it took place on February 9th – my ninth birthday. Disney fans may like to know that the highest-grossing Broadway production of all time, *The Lion King*, had its very first performance at the Orpheum in July 1997. The theatre has a capacity of over twenty-five hundred.

Crossing the street from the Orpheum, we took the first left and headed down South 10th Street to our next stop, which was at 1010 Nicollet Mall, three blocks down. The Dakota Jazz Club has been at this location since 2003 and – despite its name – is an intimate fine-dining venue that hosts not just jazz, but all types of performers, from rock and pop to cabaret. The club's unassuming entrance is through a revolving door located at the foot of an escalator in the adjoining mall. The Dakota was one of Prince's favourite haunts in Minneapolis – famed for its cocktails and superb chef-driven menu – and he often snuck in through a side door unannounced to watch artists perform. It's been said that he visited the Dakota at least once a month when he was home.

Prince played six low-key shows at the Dakota over three nights

– two shows per night – from 16th to 18th January 2013, only announcing the shows the day before. All six performances sold out within thirty minutes of going on sale causing the Dakota's website to crash, and at each brilliant show Prince dug deep into his extensive back catalogue playing rare cuts and surprise covers of Janet Jackson and Jackson 5 songs that thrilled each lucky audience of just two hundred and fifty people. A seventh show on 19th January saw Prince perform a mini sampler set before performing a drum solo and spinning records with DJ Rashida.

On the 19th April 2016, Prince spent the evening at his private table on the second floor, watching a performance by Lizz Wright. Sadly, it was to be his last visit to the Dakota Jazz Club. Prince passed away just two days later. Upon hearing the news, the club placed a single purple flower on Prince's table – #299 – with a card reading 'Rest in peace, Prince'. Before that evening's performance began, soft purple light shone across the stage in a mark of quiet respect to the fallen superstar. The club has kept Prince's table open ever since. It is – they say – *his* table.

We took photos and headed back to First Avenue and 7th St Entry.

While we waited outside First Avenue for our tour to begin, I began talking to a young girl named Rachel who was standing inside the lobby. She was friendly and welcoming and she told me that she worked on the merchandise stall at the club. We chatted about Prince's music for a few minutes, and I pointed out that she was wearing a Waxahatchee t-shirt, a band whose music I was familiar with. Rachel told me that the band had played at the club the previous night. I talked about my work at the record store back in England and she laughed, saying that she worked in a local music retailers too. I looked outside and saw that a crowd was gathering on the sidewalk for our tour, so I said goodbye to Rachel and told her I might speak to her later.

Our tour guide was a good-natured guy named Randy Hawkins. An impressive twenty-eight year veteran of First Avenue, he had worked as a sound technician in the club as well as managing and playing in several Minneapolis bands. He began by telling us a little about his role at First Avenue and said that this was his first day as a tour guide and we were his very first party. He jokingly apologised that he would try his best to answer our questions, but wasn't "That great a Prince fan, really."

Someone shot back with a laugh, "Then find someone who is!"

After pointing out the features of the exterior of the club, we finally ventured inside the building where the *Purple Rain* movie was set.

The first thing I noticed was that the club wasn't particularly big, and it was easy to imagine how jumping the place must have been when it was packed to the rafters during filming of the movie in 1983. There were only around thirty people in our tour party and it already felt like there were a lot of people in the room.

The interior of First Avenue had an industrial feel to it with a plethora of steel staircases and railings, and other than the air-conditioning ducts in the ceiling and the seating, almost every other surface in the place was a shade of black. The look was total new wave and punk. Halfway up the right staircase as we looked toward the stage was Joe Cocker's star, dated 4/3/70, the date he opened The Depot. Not to be outdone, on the opposite balcony, was another star for Prince, with the date 7/27/84 on it, the date that the *Purple Rain* film opened in movie theatres. It looked down over the imposing raised performance area and enormous lighting rig which took up a surprisingly large part of the room. The railed balconies on three sides offered brilliant views of the action. As we looked up from the main floor in front of the sound desk, I recalled the dancers in the movie on the balcony during the musical numbers, and smiled to myself. It really didn't look like much of the decor had changed in the four decades since *Purple Rain* was shot, and as our party stood on it, we remarked to each other that the now worn original checkerboard floor in the main room was a great reminder of a bygone era.

On the balcony to the right – as you faced the stage – were the restrooms where a woman once reportedly committed suicide.

A member of our party asked Randy whether anyone has seen her ghost. Randy confirmed that people have claimed so, and said that he doesn't like to be alone in the club after dark. The restrooms were decorated in '80s black and blue tiles with stainless steel fittings. Taking photos, I imagined The Revolution and The Time – Prince's protégés – hanging out in there in the early '80s.

Suddenly, it was the moment we had been waiting for. Randy informed us that we were allowed to stand on the stage. This was the most exciting part of the tour for all of us and hundreds of photos were taken as everyone got their moment to stand on this hallowed spot, which was so crucial to the Prince story. Understandably, everyone present wanted to be on the stage alone. This included me, Jonathan, and Ben. When I eventually got that moment, I was thrilled to be standing on the actual stage where the title track from the *Purple Rain* movie – and arguably Prince's most famous song – was committed to tape. It's not a commonly known fact, but the single version of 'Purple Rain' that you might know – that everyone who has ever heard it knows – is actually a live performance recording made on this spot.

Being on First Avenue's revered stage was an emotional moment for us all and in rather comedic fashion we took a ridiculous amount of time to begrudgingly leave the platform. It was far longer than Randy would have liked and we forgot that the poor guy had a time limit to stick to. As we finally left the stage, Jonathan spied a rack with copies of that week's *City Pages* on it with an article ranking Prince's studio albums inside. He grabbed a few copies of the free publication, and we stuffed them into our bags.

We headed toward the backstage area, and Randy pointed out the recently unearthed original handwritten "scribble strips" for Prince and The Revolution that were still there on the sound processor units at the side of the stage. Historically, a space was provided on the front of such equipment allowing sound engineers to note which instrument or musician was allocated to each channel for recording or live performance purposes. It's done electronically these days. The sight of these original paper ones taped to the consoles drew audible gasps from our party, and we scrambled to get good photos of the names that had been there for almost thirty-five years. Every member of The Revolution was there. I even spotted Susan Rogers' name and realised that this was clearly from the recording of the songs used for the *Purple Rain* soundtrack. Susan was Prince's principle engineer for many years. I looked at the names written on the strips and blinked, wondering if my eyes were deceiving me. They weren't. It was real. I realised that I was looking at actual musical history. Some of the songs I have loved since childhood – and from arguably one of the biggest albums of all time – were made right here.

As we toured the backstage area and the dressing rooms, we saw that they were surprisingly compact and basic. The walls were painted olive green and photographs of past performers and staff members were dotted about the walls. Prince was there, of course. In fact, he was everywhere. His presence permeated the building entirely, and everyone there could feel it. While we crowded into the tiny room looking around and taking more photographs, Randy threw up fascinating anecdotes and pointed out items of interest.

After seeing the tiny 7th St Entry side-bar and standing on its small sunken stage, we congregated in the club's loading-in dock, out back. Period graffiti littered the concrete walls and Prince's name and symbols were everywhere. This is the part of music venues I always enjoy seeing the most. I get to see quite a few of these areas with my job. It's a part of rock performance spaces that the public generally don't get to see, and they're nearly always the same regardless of how prestigious the building may be. The thought that genuine rock superstars of Prince's stature must pass through these often quite shabby portals always amuses me.

One wall above the door stated in hastily scribbled pencil, 'Prince walked thru here! 07/07/07' and I didn't doubt it for a second. We headed back inside to the VIP balcony at the opposite end of the main room from the stage.

Entry to this section of seating was through a little gate stating,

'Owner's Area', and we were permitted to sit in the red velvet upholstered chairs that were there, overlooking the stage. One was the club owner's chair which Prince occasionally used as it was apparently his favourite spot to watch bands play. It had a brass plaque on the back bearing the legend, 'Reserved for the Boss'. I noted while sitting in it that the view of the stage from this vantage point was unrivalled.

After eighty minutes inside First Avenue, we headed toward the exit as the next tour party entered the main room. I chatted to Rachel on the merchandise stall for ten minutes and spent a hundred and fifty dollars on First Avenue goodies. Our day in the Twin Cities was off to an incredible start and we headed outside, blinking in the bright sunlight. We ducked into The Depot and I picked up an ink drawing of First Avenue from behind the bar and a couple of American women asked us if we'd like to spend the day with them. I politely declined and we were off.

417 1st Avenue North – a block south of Butler Square – was the site of The Guitar Shop, where Prince used to hang out at as a young boy. Together with childhood friend André Anderson – later André Cymone – the future rock star would jam on the instruments in the back room of Charles 'Chuck' Orr's store. Chuck – a luthier – eventually went on to make Prince's first custom guitar and matching bass as the young musician began his journey to becoming a household name. A few years later, Prince thanked Chuck for his work by giving him a signed glossy headshot dedicated to 'The greatest guitar maker in the world'. I learned later that Chuck passed away in April 2005. The store no longer exists and we had trouble locating the exact spot where it used to be, so I spoke to a lady in a nearby army surplus store – Jumpwings Heritage Brands – at 327 1st Avenue North. She hadn't heard of The Guitar Shop or Chuck Orr, so I assumed it hadn't been at that location for a considerable length of time. We eventually found the spot – a totally unremarkable building – and rested there for a while.

Our next stop was approximately one mile away at 761 Washington Avenue North. We had a leisurely walk to this location taking photographs of numerous buildings and the Metro Blue Line light rail system, and we talked excitedly about the things we had seen so far. The Blue Line is comparable to the tramway systems some cities in the UK have. On the way to Washington Avenue, we took a couple of wrong turns and on more than one occasion a friendly Minneapolitan stopped to help us out. After twenty minutes we arrived at our destination.

Bunkers Music Bar and Grill was a traditional American bar and diner serving burgers until one in the morning. It offered music lovers the opportunity to see live performers every night of the week in an informal and relaxed setting. Prince performed at Bunkers ten times in total from 1989 to 2010, mainly with members of the New Power Generation and long-time associate Margaret 'Margie' Cox. Cox, a Minneapolis native from the age of seven, is a skilled multi-instrumentalist who recorded many songs with Prince in the early nineties, some of which remain unreleased at the time of writing.

From 1995 until 1999, Prince performed at Bunkers under his Love Symbol moniker but he never played at the club as a headline act. Instead, eight of the ten shows were simply billed as the regular house band, Dr Mambo's Combo – now just the Legendary Combo – a soul and R&B group who had played at the venue since 1987. The remaining two Bunkers shows Prince performed at were as the guest of Sheryl Crow in 1999, and Kip Blackshire in 2004. The NPG's powerhouse drummer Michael Bland – who was an associate of Prince for seven years – was discovered and hired by Prince while playing in Dr Mambo's Combo. NPG bassist Sonny Thompson – aka Sonny T – was also once a member. Margie Cox was one of the original members from 1987, and she is still in the band today. She appeared on the 1994 *1-800-NEW-FUNK* Prince compilation LP covering his track 'Standing at the Altar', which was released as a single. We grabbed a drink at Bunkers before heading off to our next stop which was back in the direction we had come.

In October 1990, Prince opened Glam Slam, a prime music venue and nightclub in the Minneapolis Warehouse District at 110 North 5th Street. The club – named after the second single from his 1988 *Lovesexy* album – featured paintings by Brian Canfield Mitchell and an interior-to-die-for which was designed by Prince himself, rumoured to have cost two million dollars to develop. Featuring an upstairs VIP section, and many luxurious fixtures and fittings, it was billed as *the* place to be in Minneapolis. Despite being affiliated with Prince, and incorporating a boutique store selling many Prince-branded items, and the possibility of catching him tear through a blistering set onstage with his band on any given night – as Prince was prone to do – the club struggled to compete with – of all places – Prince's old stomping ground, First Avenue, which was just three blocks away. As time went on, he saw the Glam Slam venture as a liability. Prince eventually sold Glam Slam to his former bodyguard and business manager Gilbert Davison, who re-launched the club as Quest. Sadly, it too closed, after a fire in 2006. The beautiful light-grey stone building cut an imposing sight on North 5th Street, and though it was now used as office space, it was easy to see what a cool nightspot it would have been back in the nineties.

We posed for photographs next to the door that once had a neon yellow Prince symbol above it, and as I stood outside the entrance at the right end of the building, I peered through the dark glass and up the long corridor to the office workers busying themselves beyond, and wondered if many – or indeed any – of them knew the building they worked in once housed Prince's club.

We were approaching the halfway point in our first day of exploring Prince's Minneapolis and by now I was starting to feel quietly confident about our ability to see everything we had hoped to find. We didn't want to take anything for granted though, so we made a joint decision to skip lunch and carry on with our itinerary. The next stop was a bit tricky as I was unable to find any information about the precise location – other than its address –

so I would have to rely on my memory of the *Purple Rain* movie to find it.

In *Purple Rain* there's a scene where Prince is looking in the window of a store in a shopping mall, when he is approached by the movie's female protagonist, Apollonia. It's the first time they have spoken, and Prince asks for the gold chain on her boot before they leave the mall.

This scene was shot on the skyway level of the Crystal Court lobby in the IDS Center skyscraper located at 80 South 8th Street. It's the tallest building in Minnesota at over seven hundred feet and is easily recognisable, but it was so huge I was worried that we wouldn't be able to locate the exact spot from *Purple Rain*.

Fortunately, we entered the building at the right entrance to find ourselves in the Crystal Court. The incredible ceiling was a complex honeycomb of white steel and glass. It really was breathtaking. A waterfall cascaded seven storeys down to the food court. Scenes from *The Mary Tyler Moore Show* were shot in the Crystal Court in the '70s and diners could sit at her table at Basil's Restaurant. We rode the same escalator that Mary did up to the skyway level, and I looked around to see if I recognised the spot from the movie. After a minute or two I had it. We looked across to our left at the Wells Fargo Bank and I knew that this was the location. I walked over and stood at the very corner of the balcony that Prince walks past as Apollonia follows him in *Purple Rain*, and although the building was teeming with people going about their day, we managed to get a few good photographs of the spot from the movie.

While we were there, Ben used the opportunity to withdraw some cash from Wells Fargo. Feeling pleased with myself for finding our goal so easily, I went into the Love from Minnesota gift shop back on the ground floor as we were leaving, and purchased a couple of limited edition Prince prints signed by Minneapolis artist Kristi Abbott, and a new Prince biography.

From the IDS Center we crossed the street, and it was just a short walk southwest along South Marquette Avenue and then left onto

South 9th Street, where our next stop was located on the corner of 3rd Avenue South.

The original location of the Sound 80 recording studio – where Prince recorded demos for his debut LP *For You* in 1977 – doesn't exist anymore sadly, but the company still does. It now resides in the Campbell Mithun Tower at 222 South 9th Street. We thought it was still worth a look, and took a short escalator ride up to the mezzanine level. Looking around, we couldn't find Studio 80. Fortunately, we spotted a guy at an information desk who advised us that our destination was located more than thirty storeys above us.

We entered an elevator and with dizzying speed we shot up to our chosen floor. Stepping out into the corridor, it was eerily silent and we headed to Sound 80 at Suite 3600. Sadly, the production facility was closed to the public but we could see inside the offices and it looked very cool and arty. Jonathan thought he spotted someone inside so I rang the bell. I hadn't really thought about what I was going to say to whoever came to the door, but I secretly hoped that they would invite us in or perhaps recount some brilliant Prince tale that I hadn't heard before that had been passed down in company folklore.

Unfortunately, the lady who opened the door to me had no such tale to tell. Nor did she invite us in. After a brief-but-polite conversation where she apologetically revealed that she knew very little about Prince, I thanked her for her time and we were on our way.

At South 10th Street and Marquette – just a minute or two from our last stop – there was a five-storey mural on the side of a building featuring over-sized musical notes. Known as the Schmitt Mural, it depicts the work of French composer Maurice Ravel, and it is an excerpt from the technically challenging third movement – entitled 'Scarbo' – of a 1908 solo piano piece called *Gaspard de la Nuit*. It is so challenging in fact, that many music scholars regard it as one of the most difficult piano pieces in the world to play. Although the building was no longer owned by

Schmitt Music, the current occupiers decided to keep the mural in a nod to the city's musical culture and art scene.

In 1977 – a year before his debut LP *For You* was released – Prince, sporting a huge afro, bell-bottomed jeans, and a white scarf tied around his waist, was the subject of a photo-shoot in front of the Schmitt Mural. We stood on the same spot and recreated the shots from forty years prior. The original photographs of the then-nineteen-year old Prince were taken by photographer Robert Whitman, and were used in Prince's first press-kit which was sent out to record labels in a bid to secure a deal for the prodigious teen.

Our next port of call was a cab ride away on 4th Avenue South in Southern Minneapolis. While we waited for our taxi we saw a Corvette parked at the roadside. It was red, which delighted us immensely for obvious reasons. The cab ride took approximately ten minutes, and our good-natured driver pointed out buildings of interest on the way. We travelled south on Lasalle Avenue, then east on East Franklin Avenue, before arriving at a true Minneapolis landmark.

On the corner of 4th Avenue South and East Franklin – on a small street just three blocks long running parallel to the I-35W highway – was the historic Electric Fetus record store.

Founded in 1968, the store had been at its present location since 1972. Prince was a long-time patron, and he visited Electric Fetus on Record Store Day 2016, just five days before his death. Bob Fuchs, the store's retail manager told Minnesota's online news source MPR News that the six CDs Prince purchased that day were Stevie Wonder's 'classic period' 1972 album *Talking Book*, sixties soul band The Chambers Brothers' *The Time Has Come*, Joni Mitchell's *Hejira* from 1976, Swan Silvertones' *Inspirational Gospel Classics*, a Missing Persons best of, and Carlos Santana's *Santana IV*, which had just been released the day previous to Prince's visit.

As we pulled up outside the store, I spotted a Prince display in the window advertising his last two albums, and as we walked toward the door it started to rain steadily. Foolishly, I had left the umbrella in the car back at the parking lot.

I work in a record store back in the UK called Sound it Out Records. We are a popular store, but this place was on a different level. It was enormous. As we entered the premises, a staircase on the right went down into the basement, which wasn't open to customers. I used the restroom down there a while later. On the left, an enormous counter ran the full depth of the store. As I looked right across the store, it went on as far as I could see. There were displays selling jewellery, candles, rock memorabilia, books, and there was an abundance of Prince merchandise.

We checked our bags in line with store policy, and began to browse this treasure trove of music. The store sold new and second-hand records and I naturally gravitated toward the Prince section. I picked out a hard-to-find vinyl compilation of Prince cover versions and a CD box-set, and spoke to a girl called Amy who was one of the store managers. We talked for a few minutes and she gave me a card with her email address on it, and I promised to send her a DVD of the documentary that was made about the store I work in back in the UK.

The Electric Fetus was the first place on our travels that I encountered other Prince devotees in any significant number. There had been others at the tour of First Avenue obviously, but this place was a sea of purple. I spoke to lots of people from all corners of the globe, and we talked about the places we had visited that day. To my surprise, hardly anyone else was doing what we were doing. When I'd been planning our itinerary back at home, I had anticipated seeing lots of others undertaking a similar pilgrimage to the one we were on – and visiting the same landmarks that we had scheduled for our trip – but so far, we hadn't really encountered anyone. Many people we spoke to professed that they wished they'd thought of it before departing for Minneapolis.

We continued browsing the store and I picked up a couple of Prince books, which I paid for, before leaving them with our bags behind the counter while we left Electric Fetus to quickly go to the next two locations on our list, which were right nearby.

As we exited the record store, the rain was falling heavily and – without an umbrella – we decided to run to the first of Prince's childhood homes which was just a few hundred feet away in the Longfellow neighbourhood.

Heading east on East Franklin Avenue, we crossed the bridge spanning the freeway and took an immediate right onto 5th Avenue South. The street runs south alongside the busy main road that runs through Downtown Minneapolis, and it is shielded from the steep drop and constant barrage of noise coming from the non-stop traffic thundering down the freeway by a huge concrete wall.

The weatherboard houses on 5th Avenue South were pretty, but unostentatious. Many had little porches that were cluttered with bicycles, BBQs, toys, and the detritus of family life, and there on the left – just a short distance down – the next building you come to past East 22nd Street was the very first home Prince ever lived in.

2201 5th Avenue South was a large squat two storey apartment building which was currently painted a rather conspicuous salmon pink and green. Built in 1920, the paintwork had faded a little and the flat roof and tiles on the porch require some repair, but the building was still solid. I noted that the wobbly chain fence around the building could do with replacing.

By the time we got to the house, we were wet through, but the sight of this – the first place that Prince ever called home – was so exciting that I didn't care. We stood at the end of the raised concrete path leading to the entrance and strained to see inside the three little rectangular windows on the front door. We wondered aloud which room could be apartment 203 – the room Prince's parents lived in – and imagined him possibly sitting in his stroller on the stoop as an infant. The irony that the address of the record store Prince frequented throughout his adult life was within seconds of the future musician's very first abode was not lost on us.

As we stood outside this historic building taking photographs of ourselves grinning from ear to ear, I marvelled at how one of the greatest musical artists of our time came from such humble beginnings, and I felt immensely proud of Prince. I thought back to the moment we first saw the sprawling Paisley Park complex and to all the times in my life I had seen him perform live in front of adoring thousands, and now – being here where it all began – I felt a huge amount of admiration and love for this little kid who had conquered the world, and standing there in the pouring rain, I felt so close to him that I cried. By then we were saturated, but there was one more place we needed to see before heading back to the Electric Fetus and back Downtown.

Prince Rogers Nelson was born on the 7th of June 1958 at Cedars Mount Sinai Hospital in South Minneapolis. The hospital was the first non-sectarian hospital in Minnesota. After surveys showed that Jews working in the medical profession were facing discrimination and were routinely excluded, Jewish community leaders began fundraising to open a medical facility that would welcome all minorities on its staff. In February 1951, Dr. Moses Barron – a Russian by birth who had grown up in Minnesota from the age of five – opened the Cedars Mount Sinai for business. Boasting nearly two hundred beds, the facility was a modern marvel, garnering enormous civic prestige for its founders. For us though, this part of the Prince story is sadly missing one crucial detail. Cedars Mount Sinai Hospital closed in 1991. The building in which Mattie Della Shaw gave birth to one of the finest musicians the world has ever seen still stands, but we had no way of knowing which one it was amongst the several that make up the Philips Eye Institute, as it was now known. I was aware of this fact before we even set foot in America on this trip, but I included the location on our itinerary anyway, as I felt it was still an important site and definitely worth visiting.

We followed East 24th Street for three blocks to the site

adjacent to Peavey Field Park where Prince had entered the world, and quickly grabbed some photos before running the way we had come back to Electric Fetus as finally, the rain eased off a little.

We picked up our bags and I said goodbye to Amy, and as we left the record store we noticed some posters on the door informing us that two people from Prince's inner circle would be appearing there in the coming days. On Sunday 23rd April, Susannah Melvoin – Prince's ex-fiancée and one-time member of Prince protégés The Family and the expanded 1986 line-up of The Revolution – would be appearing in-store. The following day, Ida Nielsen – the bass guitarist from Prince's final band 3rdeyegirl – was scheduled to perform live and sign her new CD. Ben, a keen bass player, was particularly excited about the prospect of meeting Ida.

We made a note of the in-store times and caught a cab to take us back to Downtown, and the parking lot on South 7th Street where we had left our car at just after 9.00am that morning. In the warm taxi – shivering, wet, and extremely happy – I realised with a heavy heart that we wouldn't be going to at least one of the appearances at the Electric Fetus. While Ida was performing on Monday, we would be at the airport leaving Minneapolis. Ben hadn't realised this.

We got back to the car around 3.00pm and grabbed snacks at the convenience store located at the base of the parking garage. We set the GPS for our next stop and headed northwest. As we drove past First Avenue and 7th St Entry, we played 'When Doves Cry' on the stereo and looked at the building that had been the setting for *Purple Rain* one last time.

Heading out of town on North 7th Avenue, we passed the Target Center on our right and turned left onto Highway 55 going east, away from Downtown. As we approached the Sumner branch of Minneapolis County Library – passing the Wayman Church and Harvest Prep School – we neared our destination. At the Project for Pride in Living building, we turned left and crossed oncoming traffic on the Olson Memorial Highway and swung an immediate right onto South Frontage Road. Driving four blocks, we turned left onto North Newton Avenue, and our next stop was right there at the end of the street.

John Lewis Nelson was a jazz musician from Louisiana. He moved to Minneapolis in 1948. A piano player, John used the stage name Prince Rogers, and formed a band named the Prince Rogers Trio. Marrying Mattie Shaw, a jazz singer, in 1957, John would go on to name their son Prince Rogers Nelson in 1958.

We parked the car on the opposite side of the street and looked out of the window at the neat little white house where Prince had stayed with his father, who had purchased the house in 1972 after his separation from Prince's mother in 1969.

539 North Newton Avenue was a smart three-bedroom residence in the North Minneapolis neighbourhood of Harrison. With a footprint covering eleven hundred square feet, the house – which was built in 1904 – was pretty and featured a front porch running the full width of the property. The lot it sat on was immaculately kept with colourful flowers all around the property. At the front of the house there was a small bedroom window on the second floor.

According to legend, John L Nelson threw the only-just-teenage Prince out of this house after catching him in bed with a girl. Prince then moved in with his friend, André Anderson. Prince's father continued to live at North Newton Avenue until well into the '80s, by which time his son was a superstar. He eventually moved to a purple house in Chanhassen that belonged to Prince. After the incident with the girl, Prince and his father never lived together again. John L Nelson died in 2001 aged eighty-five. At the time of his son's death in 2016, the property on North Newton Avenue was owned by Prince. His sister, Tyka Nelson, listed the property as her address in probate filings after his passing.

As we exited the car and walked a few steps across the street to take a picture, I noticed a man coming around the side of the house toward us. At the front of the property were Hennepin

County Sheriff's Office and security company signs warning trespassers to keep away. As the man got near, I saw that he was a black guy of about my age, dressed in sweats and a casual but expensively-branded windcheater. He had a kind face, and a friendly smile. In traditional British fashion, I began to apologise for disturbing him, but he stopped me and said it was fine. He asked us if we were Prince *fam*, and we nodded that we were. He then asked where we had travelled from and when we said that we were from England, it took him by surprise.

"Man," he exclaimed, "you guys must be really big fans, huh?"

He extended his hand and we shook it in turn.

"Hi," he said, 'I'm Reese. I'm Prince's brother-in-law."

Jonathan, Ben, and I turned and looked at each other.

"You're Prince's brother-in-law?" I said, incredulously.

"Yes," said Reese smiling, "I'm married to his sister Tyka." He laughed and began to tell us about the house, and about Prince. He pointed to the upstairs window and informed us that this was Prince's room. Reese chuckled as he told the story of Prince getting caught with the girl by his father, and he affectionately called Prince a "naughty little kid".

We chatted for a while and I asked if anyone else had dropped by before us to see the house, and to our astonishment he told us that he had been at the property all day and we were the first people he'd seen.

It was around 4.00pm. The sky was starting to darken a little and the rain had started up again.

Reese asked if he could have some photographs taken with "My new friends from England," and we were more than happy to oblige. We took tons of photos and laughed as we tried to get a group shot with Reese holding my phone and trying several times – mostly unsuccessfully – to get a good one with the house in the background. Eventually, he pulled it off and took one he was happy with and we shook his hand once more before leaving.

The second we got back in the car, Jonathan checked online.

"It's him alright!" he laughed, punching the air. "Maurice 'Reese' Phillips!"

He showed me a photo of Reese wearing a cool purple suit. We were elated that we had just met a member of Prince's family. I started the car and we headed off to our next stop on this incredible day.

From 1970 to 1972 – prior to buying the property on North Newton Avenue – John L Nelson was listed in city records as living at Apartment 105, 1707 Glenwood Avenue, which was just a two-minute drive away from the house we had just left.

Heading south on North Newton, we turned left onto Glenwood and drove just two and a half blocks until we reached the building on the right side of the street. We were momentarily distracted by a mural on a building on the other side of the street and actually missed the location, which was across from Milda's Café. I turned the car around and parked. 1707 Glenwood was a dark-grey and rather brutal-looking brick construction and the inclement weather didn't help its drab appearance. We grabbed some photos and set off again to the next spot. This one had us very excited indeed.

There were two main locations central to the movie *Purple Rain*. The first was a site we had already visited today – First Avenue and 7th St Entry – and the second was the one we were on the way to. It was the house Prince's character 'The Kid' lives in with his dysfunctional family. The GPS showed us that the address – 3420 Snelling Avenue South – was a good distance away and would take approximately twenty minutes to get to.

I drove back toward Downtown Minneapolis before joining Hiawatha Avenue and travelling southeast. Leaving the highway at East 32nd Street, we travelled through the Longfellow neighbourhood and took a right turn onto Snelling, passing the Leder Bros scrap metal recycling plant.

As we approached the tree-lined avenue where the *Purple Rain* house was situated, I slowed the car down and we looked around for the property, noting that some of the homes on Snelling Avenue were beautifully painted.

As we pulled alongside the house we were looking for, it was instantly recognisable. Sitting in the car at the roadside by a large tree – which was right between the house and the neighbouring property – I looked down the street and the scene where Prince rides up to the house on his motorcycle in *Purple Rain* played out in my mind. Mercifully there was a short break in the rain and we got out of the car to take a closer look.

At that moment, a girl came out of the front door of the house to the right of the home we were there to see. She was wearing a bright pink beanie and black-rimmed glasses, and she had two beautiful Afghan Hounds by her side. I approached her, and for a moment I could see that she was slightly apprehensive. Seeing three strangers getting out of a black car on your quiet street – right outside your home, no less – must be disconcerting obviously, so I smiled and spoke to her, saying we had travelled from the UK to tour Prince's town, and upon hearing this she relaxed a little.

I introduced myself and asked her name, and she told me it was Pilar. The dogs were waiting patiently for their walk and I asked if it was okay for me to stroke them. She said it was and I did so, asking their names.

"This is Tasha and Sergeant," Pilar said.

We talked for a minute or two about the house and she told me that it had been empty for some time and was a little run-down. I asked if she knew who owned it and she said that she was pretty sure it belonged to Prince, explaining that he purchased the property roughly a year before his passing, and it now belonged to his estate. Pilar said that she remembered it being for sale. According to reports, Prince paid a hundred and seventeen thousand dollars for the house in a bid to secure it, which was seven thousand dollars over the asking price.

Pilar told us that people regularly came to look at the house and as we talked, I looked over to the wooden steps leading up to the front door. They had purple ribbons tied to the rails. The front of the house had had some minor remodelling carried out, and the door was on the left side rather than at the front as it is in *Purple Rain*, but it was essentially the same as it appears in the movie. Even the concrete steps that Prince runs up to the original front door were still there right next to the newer wooden steps, even though the door had gone. From where I was standing at Pilar's front gate, I could see that the mailbox had purple items in it that had been placed there by previous visitors. Before she left us, I asked Pilar if I could get a photograph with her and she giggled before removing her hat and glasses and throwing back her long dark hair. We posed for a photo which Jonathan took and I thanked her before she said we should take some photos of the house. She left us to have a look around the property and took Tasha and Sergeant for their exercise.

We explored the perimeter of the house and took lots of photos and I peered in the window. The interior of the property was in quite a bare state and the rear yard was a little overgrown. The famous basement window – which Prince and Apollonia climb through in *Purple Rain* – was boarded up. We spent a while posing for each other in front of the house and I looked in the mailbox. Amongst the items placed there was a pair of purple sunglasses. After a time, we decided that we should move on and we sat in the car for a minute or two looking at the house before setting off.

We needed to eat, so we agreed to find a place we had added to our itinerary that had no links with Prince, but was an establishment of local legend nonetheless. Before that though, we had one more spot today to check out and this one was tinged with sadness.

From Snelling Avenue South, we turned right and headed west on East 35th Street and I drove through the Powderhorn neighbourhood until we came to the crossing with Park Avenue South. Turning right we saw the building we were looking for on our left on the corner of Park Avenue and East 34th Street. It was the church where Prince and his first wife, Mayte Garcia, were married.

The United Methodist Church has stood on this site at 3400 Park Avenue in South Minneapolis for over a hundred years. Built in brown brick and relatively modern in appearance, this unassuming location was not a place one would associate with rock star weddings, but it was here on Valentine's Day 1996, that Prince Rogers Nelson – by this time known as the unpronounceable Love Symbol glyph brought about by his infamous spat with Warner – and Mayte Jannell Garcia, a professional belly dancer of Puerto Rican ancestry, were joined in matrimony.

With February 14th falling on a Wednesday that year, the chances of onlookers turning up to ogle the proceedings were slim. In a further bid for secrecy, the couple had tried to throw *fam* and the press off the scent claiming that they intended to marry in Paris. In reality though, Prince – like he had done so many times in his life and career – chose a location to celebrate his nuptials that was important to him back home in Minneapolis. In the end – as is the way – the media found out about the venue and on the day of Prince and Mayte's marriage, news helicopters flew overhead.

In the church, Garcia – then twenty-two – wore white Versace while her thirty-seven-year old groom looked resplendent in white bell-bottomed pants and a matching bolero jacket emblazoned on the back with his famous symbol intertwined with an added 'M' for his intended. The guest list was small, and the intimate ceremony lasted approximately forty-five minutes. During the wedding service, the accompanying music was a mix of classical pieces by Handel and Mozart, and a wedding suite Prince had composed specially for the occasion, titled *Kama Sutra*. Prince's closest friend Kirk Johnson served as his Best Man and the day's proceedings were officiated over by Kirk's brother. By candlelight – and surrounded by white and gold orchids – the couple exchanged vows and Mayte took the name Garcia-Nelson. White doves were released to celebrate their partnership. Prince and his new bride allowed the church to keep the flowers and decorations that had cost tens of thousands of dollars.

Prince had chosen the Park Avenue church as it had already

played a part in his life. According to the church, he had participated in summer ministries there as a boy, even travelling on missions on occasion. After his wedding, church staff said that Prince would sometimes quietly enter the sanctuary during worship and observe from the back, leaving quickly before he was spotted. Upon the passing of his half-brother Duane Nelson, in May 2013 Prince returned to Park Avenue UMC to attend his funeral.

We parked the car in the church parking lot and took some photos while pointing out features of the building, before driving around the perimeter of Powderhorn Park and turning right onto Cedar Avenue South.

A few minutes from Park Avenue United Methodist Church – on the corner of East 35th at 3500 Cedar Avenue South – was the legendary Matt's Bar.

Opened in 1954, this tiny beer and burger joint – where the service is cash-only – is one of two restaurants in Minneapolis claiming responsibility for the invention of the Jucy Lucy burger. Originally conceived decades ago when a customer asked for two patties with a slice of cheese between them, the Jucy Lucy has evolved into a single patty and is essentially a burger with molten cheese inside it. Dining at Matt's Bar has become an essential Minneapolis experience. In June 2014, even the-then President Barack Obama visited and enjoyed a Jucy Lucy when he was in town. Almost a year before we arrived at this spot, my friend Michael in Kansas City told me that it was imperative that we went here.

As we approached the crossing where Matt's Bar was located, we saw that there was nowhere to park the car, so we pulled onto 18th Avenue South just around the corner. Caught in a torrential downpour, we ran to the restaurant through puddles inches deep.

The streets around Matt's were silent and as the sky closed in we assumed that it would be quiet inside the small unassuming bar. We opened the door and stepped in to this little Minnesota landmark and it was *packed*. It was so busy in fact that we had to join a queue to get a table. To my right was the bar and at the end where we were standing, was a man working the grill faster than greased lightning. He shouted a *lot*.

Eventually we got a table and the waitress took our order.

"Are you guys trying the Jucy Lucy?" she asked, and we said that we were.

I asked if they were big and she joked that she normally ate three. She was tiny. Jonathan and I ordered two burgers each and Ben ordered one. She asked if we wanted a basket of fries and we said we'd take one each. She laughed and told us that one basket would be enough for all three of us. In the UK, a basket is the same size as a small bowl. Jonathan insisted on ordering two without seeing them, "Just to be on the safe side."

While we waited for our food to arrive, the three of us chatted about the things we'd seen so far. Ben proclaimed it the best day of his life, and I had to agree that the experience we'd had had been incredible. We revelled at the fact that it was still only our first full day in town. Our meal arrived and Ben and I couldn't finish a basket of fries between us. True to form, the eating machine to my right demolished both of his burgers and a full basket of fries. I found out later that the TV show *Man Versus Food* was once filmed there. I wished Jonathan had been in that day. He'd have easily given that guy a run for his money.

As we ate, I noticed a guy sitting eating a burger at the bar. I was pretty sure it was the Emmy Award-winning actor Keith David. We reasoned that he might be in town because of the first anniversary of Prince's passing, which was the day after tomorrow. I toyed with the idea of saying hello, but he was enjoying his food so I decided against it. The Jucy Lucy burgers were magnificent by the way. I can thoroughly recommend them if you're ever in town. Let them cool a little first though. I learned that mistake the hard way.

After another round of drinks, we headed back to the car, tired but incredibly happy with the day's events. To be honest, I was on cloud nine. All three of us were. The day had exceeded our wildest expectations considerably, but it had been exhausting. We decided that we should head back to the hotel and sleep as the following day was going to be just as memorable as today, and we wanted to be fresh and alert to take it all in. We'd taken hundreds of photographs so far, but a large part of tomorrow was going to be a day for our memories only. Like the similarly-worded notices that were posted at his concerts in recent years asking for cameras and phones to be left at home, we felt Prince would have liked that a lot.

We drove back to our hotel in Chanhassen and retired to our rooms. I showered and called my wife to tell her about my day. It was 1.00am back in the UK, but she had waited up for my call. After recounting our adventures while she listened intently, I asked if my three youngest children – I have five aged between twenty-two and four – were missing me. My wife laughed as she told me that our youngest son Arthur had asked her earlier if he was ever going to see me again. I laughed too, and told her to reassure him that I would be home very soon. I ended the call and drifted off to sleep for a few hours.

Waking at around midnight, I plugged my phone in to charge and sent the photos I'd taken so far to my wife back at home. I switched on the TV and flicked through the channels for a while, before falling back to sleep and dreaming of the day that was to come.

Back in 2016 when I was booking this trip, I had intended to pay my respects at Paisley Park by simply visiting Prince's studio complex in Chanhassen and leaving a message on the perimeter fence. Little did I realise it at the time, but the opportunity to get much closer to my musical hero was about to present itself, opening up a whole new perspective to my journey. In November, I heard about an official celebration of Prince's life and career that was going to take place inside his incredible home.

Celebration 2017 – scheduled to take place over four days from April 20th to 23rd – was an event taking place at Paisley Park intended to honour Prince's life and legacy. To mark the first anniversary of his passing, Prince's estate would bring together many of those who had worked with this singular talent. The event was to feature live music, presentations on his work, and revealing panels where special guests from Prince's inner circle – including musicians, creative personnel, and friends – would discuss his importance as a cultural icon and the influence he had had on their lives. Covering all aspects of his career, *Celebration 2017* would also include guided tours of the complex Prince called home, and attendees would get the opportunity to see the famous studios first hand, where dozens of musical compositions had been created. *Celebration 2017* was a dream event for a Prince *fam*, and the day they went on sale we excitedly booked tickets, thrilled that our trip would now be taking us right inside Prince's world.

THURSDAY

I woke around 5.00am after another night of broken slumber. Jet lag was playing havoc with my normal sleeping pattern. I resigned myself to the fact that I probably wouldn't be sleeping properly until I returned to England.

We'd collected our Paisley Park welcome packs from reception upon our return the previous evening. They'd arrived later than we had expected so it was a relief to finally have them. Opening the envelope with my name and room number written on it, the pack contained a letter on Paisley Park-headed paper outlining the rules of the days ahead, a beautiful photo identification pass on a purple *Celebration 2017* lanyard, and a small double-sided itinerary of events with the locations inside Prince's home in which they would be taking place. The items had been meticulously designed and I was thrilled at having official Paisley Park items with my name and photograph on them. I scanned the itinerary, and my heart leapt when I saw that we were going to see Prince's bands The Revolution, the New Power Generation and 3rdeyegirl perform live as well as his protégés The Time. I'd never witnessed The Time onstage, and the fact that we were going to see them – inside Paisley Park no less – was like a dream come true. Added to the fact that The Revolution – arguably Prince's most famous backing band – were also in attendance, it almost felt as if I would be in a re-enactment of *Purple Rain*, a thought which overwhelmed me a little. In the 2.30pm Thursday slot on the itinerary, it said 'Performance – Special Guest', and I wondered who it might be. The special guest was scheduled for that afternoon, so we wouldn't have to wait long to find out. In just a few hours, we would actually be walking through the doors of Paisley Park.

The thought of being inside Prince's home made my stomach do somersaults. I was at once both excited and hugely apprehensive. I called my wife, who told me she that could tell from my voice that I was emotional. She told me that she loved me and would be thinking about me all day. After speaking to her, I posted on social media with shaking hands confessing that I was so nervous I felt sick. Within minutes I began receiving dozens of messages from friends and family back home who knew how important this day was going to be for me. They all wished me luck and everyone told me how my trip was going to change my perception of Prince forever, and as I read their kind words I was truly overwhelmed at the love and affection my friends showed me. I sat on my bed and the tears flowed. This was it.

We had a few hours to fill before *Celebration 2017* was due to start at 11.00am, so we enjoyed a leisurely breakfast and decided to check out the mural that's painted at the rear of our hotel, on the west wall of Chanhassen Cinema. Prince reportedly visited the movie theatre a few times a month to watch new movies. The mural is by a New Zealand artist named Graham Hoete. Completed in June 2016, the purple artwork was forty feet across and the detail was amazing, featuring a headshot of Prince from his Musicology era. We took photos of each other in front of the piece before deciding to have a quick drive to Paisley Park, reasoning that there may be lots of activity going on outside the complex as excitement built for *Celebration 2017*. We weren't sure whether there was anywhere to park the car outside Paisley Park so agreed to quickly come back to the hotel afterward and make alternative arrangements for getting there a little while later.

As we passed the hotel reception on the way to the car, we saw a notice promoting a book signing by Prince biographers Alex

Hahn and Laura Tiebert, which was taking place the following afternoon between 4.00pm and 6.00pm in the conference room. Alex is responsible for writing what I consider to be the definitive account of Prince's career. He and Laura had recently completed a new book which chronicles the first thirty years of his life. Luckily, I had picked up a copy from the Electric Fetus record store. Bizarrely, Alex's original biography from 2003 was in my hotel room too. I'd taken it off the shelf literally minutes before I'd left home in England, figuring I'd need something to read on the long flight over the Atlantic. It's a really hard-to-find book now and I couldn't believe my luck at having the opportunity to get both books signed by the authors. I made a note of the time they would be at the hotel, and we set off for Paisley Park at 7801 Audubon Road.

As we approached Paisley Park, our hunch about the heavy media presence was correct. Television and radio crew were everywhere. Prince *fam* crowded the sidewalks around Paisley Park, and on one spot, a man dressed from head-to-toe in purple was even painting pictures for passers-by. Interviews with celebration attendees were taking place on the street, and there was a palpable air of excitement. I drove slowly along Audubon Road before turning the car around and heading back to our hotel.

Once we were back at the hotel, we spotted that there were shuttle buses running every couple of minutes to Paisley Park. I asked at the front desk about the possibility of getting on one of them and I was told that all the places had been taken. We decided to just hire a cab to take us. It was 10.30am so the receptionist arranged a car. Within a minute it arrived and we climbed in, delighted to see that the driver of our taxi was a woman. I made a joke about it, because somebody just *had* to. 'Lady Cab Driver' is a song by Prince from his 1982 album, *1999*.

As we travelled the few minutes back to Paisley Park our driver, Joanne – who was maybe a year or two older than me – told us she loved our accent and asked if we could understand her okay. She had a great voice and spoke exactly like Frances

McDormand's character in the movie *Fargo*. Bizarrely – and even though we were deep in America's Upper Midwest – the thought suddenly struck me that this was the first time I recalled hearing a strong Minnesotan accent on this trip. Joanne thought we were from Scotland, which amused us no end and we laughed at this familiar misconception. As natives of northern England, we get that a lot – particularly from Americans – as our regional accent is often difficult to understand.

As we approached our destination, people were climbing out of buses and cars around the perimeter of the Paisley Park complex. Joanne had different ideas though, and drove straight through the gates, stopping only momentarily to inform the security officers that came running towards us that she was bringing "These Great British fellas to see Prince." We grinned at the uniformed guard and I realised that we were now officially on Prince's property. I thought back to one of the last pictures of Prince, riding his bicycle around the complex. Taken just days before his passing, it was almost exactly a year ago from this moment on this very spot. To our surprise, the official allowed the car through and we drove right up to the gleaming white building.

Joanne asked us if we wanted picking up later and she asked for my phone number, while giving us hers.

She said, "Keep hold of it, Stuart. If you need taking anywhere, night or day, call me. I'm never more than five minutes away."

We thanked her for the ride and headed towards Paisley Park's front door.

To the left of the entrance to Prince's home was a specially-erected wall displaying *fam*-art and memorial messages which had been left by people from across the world, who had felt the need to come and pay their respects at Paisley Park since Prince's passing. It is known as the Prince 4 Ever Tribute Fence. Some of the tributes were spectacularly inventive, and in an inevitable sea of purple we spotted guitars, oil paintings, and even entire costumes amongst the written eulogies to Minneapolis' fallen star. Some messages were elegant and well thought-out, their writers clearly having planned meticulously what they wanted to convey. Other notes were simple and direct. Without exception, all were incredibly heartfelt. People on either side of me were quiet, but we were united by a common bond, lost in our thoughts while showing solemn respect to our shared idol. A man I did not know hugged me. A woman I'd never met put her hand on my shoulder. We were in this together. We are *fam*. Many people cried quietly, or held handkerchiefs to their eyes and my own emotions bubbled to the surface several times as I read messages from both youngsters and long-term followers of his career. Many of them were incredibly personal, detailing how Prince's life and music had helped heal them during times of sadness or difficulty.

As I walked the length of the fence and read, I caught my breath many times as tears fell down my face. I felt extraordinarily privileged to see this incredible tribute to the little man that means so much to us, and with a heavy heart the realisation that he has gone hit me hard. The people he has left behind – me included – were hurting and this was the first time I had been amongst them, really able to show my feelings without fear of ridicule or criticism. It felt good to cry.

The Prince 4 Ever Tribute Fence is a miraculous testament to the curative power of Prince's art. There were hundreds – if not thousands – of notes and photographs thanking him, and the security guard standing nearby tried his best to shepherd people toward the entrance to Paisley Park. He insisted that we would have as much time as we wanted to look at the fence later this weekend, but the poor guy was fighting a losing battle as people largely ignored him. Jonathan, Ben, and I secured our own tributes to the fence using tie-wraps that I'd brought from home. My message to Prince was just a simple thank you. I felt it conveyed everything I wanted to say to him.

As we waited to enter Paisley Park for the first time, the suited door personnel placed our cell phones in magnetically-sealed pouches and checked our bags. Security was super tight, and we were politely-but-firmly reminded that anyone found taking photographs inside the building would be subject to a lifetime ban from Paisley Park.

While these measures might seem a little harsh to the average sightseer, to a seasoned Prince *fam*, it was no big deal. We're used to it. I've visited Graceland in Memphis, and the security measures there had nothing on Paisley Park. Having witnessed Prince perform live many times over the years, his legendary loathing of unofficial recordings and photography – particularly in the last decade of his life – was nothing new to me and – like every other *fam* – I deeply respected Prince's wishes and accepted it unequivocally. In fact, I have to say that as an avid concert-goer, attending a Prince show in the latter period of his career was always a refreshingly different experience to shows by other artists. Being in a room full of people enjoying a mesmerising performance by our musical hero – and seeing it with our own eyes rather than focusing attention on a camera lens pointing at the action – always gave me a real feeling of unity with my fellow Prince *fam*. Like the ubiquitous notices at his shows asking us to leave cameras and phones at home, these events really were *for our memories only*. Whenever I saw those notices, I knew it was going to be a special night.

The moment was upon us. Finally – after months of excitement – at 11.00am on the eve of the anniversary of Prince's passing, I stepped inside his house and began a journey that would create a new set of memories that I will carry with me forever. I'd waited nearly my whole life for this and – writing from my memory now – it's as clear to me as it was at that moment. *I am still there.*

Standing in the portico that leads into the main lobby of Paisley Park, I looked up to the balcony above me, to the spot where Prince is standing in the photo on the rear sleeve of *Art Official Age*, one of the two albums he released on the same day in September 2014. The pristine white entrance was flooded with natural light from the skylight and three large square windows that were above me.

Moving forward I was greeted by a Paisley Park staffer who checked my photo identification pass and ushered me into the building proper. The purple rug I was standing on had the Paisley Park logo on it in lilac. As I walked into the lobby, it was modestly-sized and I looked to my left. A huge window looked out over the adjacent matching oval building that stood alongside the main structure. I could see that the window was tinted so that visibility from the outside looking in was minimised. In front of me and slightly to the left there was a small reception desk like the one you would find in any hotel with attendants behind it. I looked down at the carpet and noted that it was a light grey in this reception area but changed as you entered the building proper to a beautiful powder blue with creamy-yellow crescent moons, circles, and stars placed seemingly at random. Bizarrely, upon seeing it I was worried it would get worn and dirty by so many visitors. It was a strange thought, I know, but it was the first one I had. The second was that the paintwork in the lobby was to-die-for.

The room I was standing in was painted in two subtle shades of purple. Around the ceiling perimeter was a small soffit, and the fascia board featured a meticulous hand-painted piano keyboard. It was a gorgeous little detail and I liked to think that it was an acknowledgement to Prince's pianist father and his musical heritage. Soft purple light was diffused from above the soffit creating a calming aura, and the ceiling beyond that featured an incredible interstellar vista set against a deep blue clear night. Again it was the work of skilled artisans and the attention to detail was breath-taking. It was a job of such painstaking care and accuracy that I felt like I was actually looking out into the real night sky. As I stood on that spot, the thrill I got from knowing that Prince walked here every day was indescribable, and it was all I could do to stop myself grinning from ear-to-ear. Jonathan and Ben were similarly lost, in awe at our surroundings, and it was about to get even better.

Directly in front of us as we entered Paisley Park's main building was a long corridor with lots of rooms branching off to the left. The rooms were separated by huge pillars, each of which was painted a different block of solid bold colour.

Immediately to the right before we got to them was a staircase up to the living quarters. We were not allowed there. At the foot of the staircase a hand-painted Prince lyric floated along the wall. The handrails around the upper floor featured black metalwork with symmetrical patterns. A painted mural of Prince's unpronounceable glyph was above the arched entrance to the corridor and a pair of eyes – presumably his – looked down at visitors to his home. A divine light beamed down from the mural onto us. The walls were hand-painted sky-blue with clouds dotted around on them. Again, the paint job was incredible, and it was like looking up at the sky on a beautiful summer's day. On the right wall of the staircase, there were multiple framed gold and platinum discs from Prince's entire career commemorating his sales achievements. Jonathan tried to count them, but lost it somewhere in the thirties.

As I walked under the arch, I looked to my left and there, on the wall in a small frame, was a letter of condolence written by the-then US President Barack Obama on official Whitehouse-headed paper. I stopped to read it. It was signed in purple ink. Next to it was Prince's favourite guitar.

The HS Anderson 'Mad Cat' guitar looked to be the original flamed maple one with the leopard-print strap and matching pick guard that Prince played throughout his career. Prince used this guitar in the masterful solo he played during the star-studded band performance of The Beatles' 'While My Guitar Gently Weeps' at his 2004 induction into the Rock and Roll Hall of Fame. The phenomenal performance clip is available online for anyone who may not have seen it. It's been called one of the greatest guitar solos in history, and it's hard for me to argue with that. Instantly recognisable to Prince *fam* and anyone who has seen him perform live, the guitar is worn and battered and as I stood looking at it I realised that this trip would likely be the last time I ever saw it in the flesh. I longed to touch it, but it was in a glass case so I could not, and sadly I said a silent goodbye to Prince's beloved instrument.

As I moved past the guitar, I entered the Atrium. Cosier than

I expected, it was a beautiful space and was reportedly Prince's favourite part of the building. Above me, four huge square skylights allowed the sunlight to cascade into the Atrium, and the doors to various rooms around me all featured Prince's image on them from different eras of his career. Some of the rooms had names. I couldn't see what was in them, but I was dying to find out. Outside one of the rooms was a beautiful flower sculpture. I think it was of lilacs, and I suddenly realised that that was what the whole of Paisley Park smelled of; lilac and lavender. The floor of the Atrium was tiled with a white-grey marble or similar material and the ubiquitous Love Symbol was emblazoned on it in black granite. There were some features of the Atrium that I didn't spot yet.

We were ushered through this area by tour guides who were eager to get everyone through as a backlog of bodies was occurring behind us, and they wanted us to continue quickly so the day's planned events could begin. With approximately two thousand people in attendance, you had to feel for them as they tried to keep everyone moving. It couldn't have been easy, given our surroundings. As I was carried forward by the crowd, my eyes were everywhere, trying to take all of this amazing building in. The tour guides sensed mild panic amongst us, this huge party of visitors who were thrilled to be standing inside Prince's home, and reassuringly they told us not to worry as we'd get a chance later in the *Celebration 2017* weekend to see all of this and much more. I walked past more of Prince's famous guitars on my right and a small restroom, and headed through another arch above me featuring Prince's symbol in gold on a purple background.

The next room was the Piano Room, for obvious reasons. It contained Prince's Schimmel Pegasus grand piano. It looked like no piano on Earth. Resembling a gleaming black spaceship, it was without a doubt the most outrageous-looking musical instrument I have ever seen. Featuring an ergonomically designed keyboard – the actual keys are *curved* – this organic work of art designed by Professor Luigi Colani was simply breathtaking. Customised with a revolving gold Love Symbol atop it and an integrated fully adjustable hand-stitched leather seat, its luscious black form drew gasps from everyone in the room. Less than twenty were ever built, and it is worth hundreds of thousands of dollars. To the right of the piano was a set of double doors. A sign on the wall stated that admittance was strictly by invitation and the familiar 'No cameras allowed' policy was present. Beyond these doors was a room that almost made my jaw hit the floor.

Paisley Park's Soundstage was astounding. I'd seen shows that had been recorded in this space on TV, but they hadn't conveyed the sheer size of the room I was standing in right now, and nothing had prepared me for the sight of the 12,500 square foot performance space. The room was 120 feet long and 102 feet wide, and with a height of forty five feet which could handle 2000lbs of rigging, the house lighting inventory comprised some 400 pieces of equipment. Standing in it, it simply defied belief that this room was inside his house.

The Soundstage is comparable in size to the concert hall Sage One in the UK. The acoustically tuneable performance platform was enormous, easily able to accommodate the biggest bands with a mountain of equipment. Four foot high, the stage could be patched to all of the studios on-site to allow live multi-track recording. If other artists were using the studios while a performance was taking place, it wouldn't be an issue as the entire arena was soundproofed. As I looked across the stage, it was packed with equipment including instruments, sound processors, amps, and effects pedals. In short, it was a musician's dream.

It was on this stage that Prince allegedly spoke his final words to *fam*. A few days before his passing, he appeared before them at a dance-party, reportedly saying, "Wait a few days before you waste any prayers." As I stood in front of the stage, I couldn't help but think of this.

In the past, Prince – and other artists – had used the Soundstage for live performances, tour rehearsals, video shoots, and even movie production. The '90s *Graffiti Bridge* film – the spiritual follow-up to *Purple Rain* – was shot almost entirely in this room, including indoor and outdoor scenes. Large portions of the 1987 concert movie *Sign o' the Times* were also shot here, as was 1999's New Year's Eve pay-per-view special *Rave Un2 The Year 2000*. The movies *Drop Dead Fred* and *Grumpy Old Men* were also produced at Paisley Park. Tour rehearsals took place in the Soundstage for every tour of Prince's career from 1988, and many of the incredible productions I saw him in over the years had their genesis right here, in this very room. Other artists that had utilised this space include the Bee Gees, Neil Young, Beastie Boys, and even legendary show business entertainer Barry Manilow, who I had the pleasure of seeing live in 2016 as part of his farewell tour. Looking around me at this amazing space I was totally awestruck, and it felt like I was standing in a piece of my own history as a lover of Prince's music for over thirty years. All around me people were visibly taken aback by the sheer vastness of the Soundstage. Some laughed with their friends saying, "We finally made it!" Others stared wide-eyed in disbelief and some got hugely emotional, clearly feeling blessed to be in the spot where so many memorable performances throughout Prince's career took place. I saw one lady – who I would later find out had travelled from New Zealand – and she was in floods of tears and struggling to control her breathing. Lots of attendees were dressed in flamboyant attire and I even spotted a woman wearing a suit with clouds on it. Prince wore the same in the promotional video for the 1985 single 'Raspberry Beret'. In the back corner of the auditorium – looking left from the stage – a huge Prince Love Symbol – twenty feet tall and constructed from dozens of light bulbs – hung to remind us whose house this was. To the left of it was an enormous portrait of Prince against a bright white moon. He looked down over the proceedings approvingly.

We stood in this breathtaking performance space taking it all in, and as the room began to fill with people, we took our seats on the very last row at the back figuring we could see everything from there. Behind me, a raised platform had a number of seats on it and I remarked to Jonathan and Ben that they must be reserved for special guests. I wondered who they might be. A hush slowly descended over the room. We were minutes from the start of *Celebration 2017*, and as an official took to the stage, I looked over my shoulder to see that Prince's immediate family were sitting just ten feet behind me.

Our first host of *Celebration 2017* was an unassuming looking man. He was dressed casually in sports jacket and black jeans and he addressed the audience, telling us that we were making history and that this was the first of many celebrations to be held at Paisley Park. We applauded and he introduced himself as Joel Weinshanker.

I recalled reading somewhere that this unpretentious guy was the owner of Elvis Presley Enterprises, Inc and was in charge of Graceland's tour operations in Memphis. I've been to Elvis' home and I've seen how respectful and well-executed tourist operations are there, and this thought relaxed me. We were clearly in safe hands. Joel told us that we would shortly be seeing the first concert at Paisley Park in over a year, and that he hoped we would enjoy what was going be an incredible experience. Telling the audience he was a huge Prince *fam* and was as excited as the rest of us to be there, Joel continued by saying that we were "United in our love for Prince," and informed us that throughout the four days he would be amongst attendees answering questions about the planned events and asking us for feedback so organisers of *Celebration 2017* could iron out any teething problems for future events. He said that Prince would be overwhelmed by the love in the room and promptly dropped the bombshell we had all been waiting for. He revealed who would be performing in the 'Special Guest' slot later today. It was to be none other than the legendary funk pioneer George Clinton and his band Parliament-Funkadelic. George appears in Prince's final movie *Graffiti Bridge*, and was a huge influence on Prince as a teenager. The audience went wild at this amazing news and Jonathan, Ben and I couldn't help but grin at each other. I could hear Prince's immaculately-dressed siblings applauding behind me and I turned around to watch them. One of his half-sisters caught my eye and smiled at me and I smiled back. My heart leapt. Things had been underway for mere minutes and I was already on another planet. Joel then informed us that he was not the main host for *Celebration 2017*, saying that such a special occasion demanded someone far more suitable. He invited the next official to the stage. It was Damaris Lewis, Prince's close friend and dancer since 2012.

Damaris worked extensively with Prince as part of his touring group and she performed with him at the series of critically-acclaimed shows he played at the iconic Montreux Jazz Festival in 2013. A statuesque beauty of West Indian descent, Damaris has supermodel looks. She cut a striking figure on the stage and she spoke slowly and eloquently about Prince, and about us. She started by saying that she had intended to come out and request a minute of silence as a mark of respect to Prince but instead, she asked that we held a minute of applause as it was a more fitting thank you for the wonderful legacy he has left for us all. The audience began clapping and cheering and within seconds every one of the two thousand-strong audience was up on their feet. It was an incredibly moving moment and we were unified in our appreciation of the man who has affected all of our lives. Understandably, emotions were running high and Paisley Park staffers anticipated this, handing out tissues to dry tears. The tissues were purple, of course.

Damaris called this gathering a "Purple party", and said solemnly, "It is up to us to continue his legacy. If you love Prince, you are part of that legacy."

It was a theme she returned to throughout the four days we were at Paisley Park, stressing the importance of keeping his memory – and his work – alive for generations to come.

"I really want everyone to know that when you're here, you're one," she told us. She also repeated a mantra every time she was on stage over the coming days, and it was simply "Listen. Learn. Teach. Love."

It was a message I found myself repeating for days after.

Our photo identification passes had large capital letters stamped on them and we now found out why. Damaris informed us that we were to be split into smaller parties of about forty people – each corresponding to the letter on our passes and each having its own tour guide – and we were to move around Paisley Park within these groups allowing everyone to see all of the events in turn. We were in group C. Before we met up in these groups however, we were about to see a film that had never been seen before in public.

Damaris Lewis left the stage, the lights went down, and we watched a clip from Prince and 3rdeyegirl's blistering performance at the Ziggo Dome in Amsterdam from 25th May 2014. The film was professionally shot and edited, and the audience was thrilled that this had never been seen by anyone other than Prince's inner circle before. It's a well known rumour amongst *fam* that Prince had virtually every show he ever performed professionally recorded, and watching this film it was easy to imagine them being officially released at some point in the future. There were whispers in the audience that there might be a DVD of this performance available at *Celebration 2017*, and everyone was singing along and clapping as if we were actually at the live show in Amsterdam.

The film showcased what an incredible performer Prince was. It began with 1982's 'Something in The Water (Does Not Compute)' and 'Pretzelbodylogic' from the *Plectrumelectrum* album from 2014. The band was in outstanding form before Prince took to the stage alone and performed a medley at the piano that included some of his most memorable ballads. 'How Come U Don't Call Me Anymore' segued into the sumptuous 'Condition of The Heart' – which is one of my all-time favourite Prince compositions – before morphing into 1991's 'Diamonds and Pearls', and the incredible *Purple Rain* number, 'The Beautiful Ones'. Again, it's a personal favourite. Prince's performance was stunning and it was clearly a precursor to the final *Piano & A Microphone Tour* he undertook shortly before his passing.

There was hardly a dry eye in the house at this point and suddenly there was a deliciously cruel-but-funny moment when the screen faded to black after forty-five minutes and the house lights slowly came up. We let out a collective groan at having this magical show snatched from us, but it was good-natured and everyone began to laugh. What torture! With that, the audience began to disperse and meet with team leaders, before exiting the Soundstage to watch various events around Paisley Park. I watched Prince's siblings leave quickly before anyone had a chance to approach them.

For our first panel discussion we were to remain in the Soundstage at Paisley Park. We moved closer to the front of the auditorium and took our seats right near the stage and a tingle of excitement ran through me when the words 'NPG Panel 1989 – 2000' appeared on the huge screen at the back of the stage. Then – to rapturous applause – a group of musicians I hadn't seen for nearly twenty years walked quietly onto the stage, waving to the audience as they did so. They took their seats and were introduced by the first of several interviewers throughout *Celebration 2017* who were from KCMP, a Minnesota Public Radio station known as The Current.

Levi Seacer Jr was the first to be introduced. Prince's touring bassist since the disbanding of The Revolution in the mid-'80s, Levi was a founding member of The New Power Generation in 1991, where he switched from bass to guitar. He remained with Prince until 1993, before leaving to work as a producer for the Grammy Award-winning Minneapolis/St Paul vocal ensemble Sounds of Blackness amongst others.

Seated next to Levi was Morris Hayes, Prince's former Musical Director and keyboard player with The NPG for over a decade. Morris also spent time with Minneapolis band Mazarati, a group formed by former Revolution bassist Mark Brown, or 'Brown Mark' as he is known to *fam*. Prince gave a bluesy demo version of 'Kiss' to Mazarati in 1986 before reclaiming it and turning into a worldwide hit. He softened the blow by writing and co-producing their hit '100 MPH'. Morris also enjoyed a spell touring with Prince-protégés The Time. Incidentally Mazarati also lost out on the song 'Jerk Out', which was re-recorded by The Time in 1990, becoming their biggest hit. Morris is now an in-demand actor, producer, and composer.

Anthony Mosley was next. Known as Tony M, he is a rapper who first appeared as a dancing extra in the *Purple Rain* movie in 1984. Touring with Prince in a dance troupe called The Gameboyz, he then became a full member of The NPG. Tony made a sizeable contribution to the 1991 album, *Diamonds and Pearls* and he continues to perform today.

Finally, Damon Dickson is a dancer, choreographer, and actor. He appeared in *Purple Rain* alongside Tony and – like the other members of the panel – he is a member of the newly resurrected New Power Generation, who at the time of writing, were touring, having recently supported Phil Collins.

The panel began by talking individually about how they began their association with Prince, and recounted details of their auditions for the band. Frequently humorous and startlingly revealing, these tales showed Prince to have a playful sense of humour. He was a man who was clearly fond of pranks. It was evident from the way they talked about him that they all loved Prince dearly, and they laughed amongst themselves as they told us stories about how funny Prince was, and how his incredible work ethic was a wonder to behold, and suddenly it was our turn to laugh when Morris announced in a deadpan manner that he used to call Prince "Bruh" when his bandleader declared he wanted to be known by the unpronounceable Love Symbol in the '90s.

Morris – who is incredibly witty – also talked about how Prince was an incredibly disciplined musician and expected his band to have the same dedication. He told how they would rehearse incessantly, sometimes learning songs that they often wouldn't even play at shows, and how Prince would change set lists at the last minute, always keeping the band on their toes.

Every member of the New Power Generation spoke with great affection, and they told us how Prince always motivated them to be the very best that they could be, striving to do the best job they could, always maintaining the appearance and mannerisms of a star. They also spoke of how Prince had incredible vision about the direction in which he had wanted to take the band.

As I listened to them speak about their fallen bandleader, it was amazing to see that these members of Prince's inner circle were clearly as in awe of the man as we were, and they expressed gratitude to have shared the limelight with their musical hero.

All too soon the discussion came to an end and as the interviewer wrapped up this portion of *Celebration 2017*, the members of Prince's former band graciously thanked the audience and we applauded as they left the stage. We had a few minutes before the next event and as we waited for the room to clear, I spotted Randy Hawkins, our tour guide from First Avenue and 7th St Entry. Our next panel took place next door – to the left of the stage – in the private nightclub that was inside Prince's home. That's right, the *nightclub*.

The NPG Music Club is a 200 capacity club in Paisley Park that has played host to intimate shows by Prince and many special guests. Originally the club was known as 'Love4oneanother', and in the late '90s Prince would often hold free after-show parties here, the gigs often beginning after 2.00am and continuing until the break of dawn.

These events – nearly always announced just hours before Prince hit the stage – became a regular occurrence for lucky *fam* who were treated to the incomparable spectacle of a musical superstar performing in incredibly informal surroundings. To be present at these shows must have been surreal for the privileged few who attended them, and standing there then it made me wish I'd been born a Minneapolitan. The club features a small stage and memorabilia was all around us. As we took our seats, I spotted the front end of a Cadillac – complete with grille and headlights – hanging on a wall and to my absolute joy I realised that it was the very same one from the cover of the 1987 *Sign o' the Times* album.

The screen behind the stage displayed the words 'Prince Interactive' and the guest speakers were welcomed to the intimate platform. They were Jeff Munson, Chuck Hermes, Sam Jennings, and Jeremy Gavin.

Jeff served as Prince's Art Director at Paisley Park, and he explained that during his time there – from 1988 to 1994 – he performed a number of duties from manning the front desk through the night, to designing the album sleeve for the 1993 album *Come* and starting Prince's in-house Graphic Design department. From creating logos and typography to designing book layouts and film sets, Jeff has had a hand in some of Prince's most iconic imagery. He told us the story of how he first visited Paisley Park, bringing his friend Dave Friedlander – who was working there as a sound engineer – a sandwich for his lunch. Dave showed Prince some of Jeff's designs, and he was in. With an office underneath Prince's living quarters at Paisley Park – and with a boss always willing to give him free rein to come up with new ideas – Jeff told us how he was able to live his dream of working for a musician he had loved since his youth.

Chuck Hermes was employed at Paisley Park chiefly as a Graphic Designer and he explained how he had introduced Prince to the concept of having an online presence, spending hours in the design office and experimenting with design software and graphics, much to Prince's delight. Chuck told how he had discussed chat rooms and meeting people online, concepts that Prince enthusiastically incorporated into his early websites.

Sam Jennings spoke about how he had been employed as a Designer and Webmaster at Paisley Park, and had been instrumental in designing Prince's various online guises throughout the '00s as well as creating album sleeves and elements of Paisley Park itself. Using slides that brought back a ton of memories for me, Sam talked us through the various online configurations Prince had used, from *Thedawn.com* in the late '90s through to later websites such as *3121.com*, and the *Prince Interactive* CD-ROM. I remembered every one of the websites and smiled as I saw the welcome pages I hadn't seen for many years.

Jeremy Gavin talked to us about his role as Art Director at Paisley Park from 2003 to 2007. Amongst his many achievements while working for Prince, Jeremy was responsible for the incredible packaging layout for the 2001 album, *The Rainbow Children*, which is among my favourite Prince sleeves. As we watched him talk about designing it, I looked to my right and the album's front cover artwork – painted by artist Cbabi Bayoc – was right there, printed on a huge curtain. Jeremy discussed Prince's use of technology and how he had embraced new practices ahead of the pack, becoming one of the most innovative artists of his generation. All four of the panellists expressed their appreciation to Prince for their time at Paisley Park and the fascinating forty minute session drew to a close before lunch.

Jonathan, Ben and I left the NPG Music Club through the rear entrance, and stepped into a large lobby to the back of the Soundstage, which was thronging with people. The merchandise stall was there, and it was already three deep as attendees rushed to purchase Prince and Paisley Park-branded items. Male and female restrooms were located to the left of the NPG Music Club's exit, and on the wall between them a large screen showed clips of Prince's live performances and music videos. The now-legendary Miami Super Bowl XLI half-time performance from 2007 featured heavily.

We stepped through a set of double doors to the right of the screen and walked into a huge marquee that had been erected for *Celebration 2017*. Four rows of tables – each fifty feet long – ran the length of the room, which was easily capable of seating several hundred people at a time. We made our way to the far end of the marquee and helped ourselves to the free lunch. On offer was pesto pasta with black rice and chickpeas, and a green salad. Dessert was a selection of cakes. It all appeared to be vegetarian – this was Prince's house after all – and this suited me fine. As I said earlier, I'm not a fan of red meat.

We grabbed some drinks and sat down to eat, talking about how amazing the day had been. The food was delicious and I went back for more. Despite the fact that we'd now been there for several hours, I still couldn't believe that we were inside Paisley

Park. I felt detached from reality. Around us I could see that others felt the same. We were allowed access to our cell phones in this area so we had the staff unlock them from their magnetically sealed pouches.

We posted excitedly on social media and texted friends and family telling them what we had been up to so far, before stepping outside into the bright Minneapolis sunshine for a while to take some photos of the building up close.

I chose this moment to call my wife at home and she answered immediately. It was around 8.00pm back in the UK. I quickly told her what had happened so far and she remarked that I sounded happy. I said that I was, and that I was having the most amazing time. She laughed and said she was pleased that I wasn't sad. I suddenly realised that she was right. I wasn't. I was elated to be here. My worries that morning about being upset had vanished. I talked to my children – they were getting ready for bed – and I told them I missed them, then I said goodbye to my wife and ended the call. We were due to head back in, so we handed our cell phones to a Paisley Park staffer who locked them up in their little bags again before handing them back to us, and we walked back into the wondrous building.

I decided to pick up some merchandise on the way back into the Soundstage, and joined the queue. I chose some books, a Paisley Park commemorative pin in the shape of the building, and a Love Symbol pendant. An American guy in front of me bought three replicas of Prince's famous Cloud guitar at a cost of fifteen hundred dollars each.

"For the kids," he said smiling.

I paid for my things, and headed back through the rear doors of the concert hall just in time to see George Clinton and Parliament-Funkadelic begin their ninety minute set.

Everybody was on their feet dancing. Onstage, George was dressed in a silver zig-zag patterned jacket and wearing a matching police officer's hat. He strutted around like a man half his age – he's seventy-five – waving a conductor's baton with glee, and he was clearly in his element. The stage was full of musicians and scantily-clad backing singers. At one point there were fifteen people on the stage.

"Put your hands together," said Clinton. "Make it funky."

By now the Soundstage at Paisley Park was in full-on party mode. As George and his band ripped through classic funk tracks like 'Atomic Dog', 'One Nation Under A Groove', 'Flash Light', and 'Give Up The Funk – Tear The Roof Off The Sucker', I stood at the rear of the room and looked back to see Damaris Lewis' long dancer's legs two feet behind my head on the platform where Prince's family were watching the show. She was dancing away – lost in the music – and as I looked up at her, she suddenly smiled at me from under her wide-brimmed hat. I turned my attention back to the stage and enjoyed the incredible spectacle of the first concert to take place in Paisley Park since Prince's passing. I feel sure he'd have approved of the choice.

After a while, I decided to visit the restroom and I pushed through the door, leaving the Soundstage. To my astonishment I walked straight into Omarr Baker – Prince's half-brother – and his female acquaintance. Omarr was wearing an incredibly sharp suit. I apologised and expressed my condolences to them both on their loss – our loss – and the immaculately-attired lady said, "Thank you."

I barely managed to keep it together until I reached the restroom and stared at my reflection in the mirror, shaking my head in disbelief. I'd been in Minneapolis for less than three full days and I'd already met two members of Prince's family. This trip was totally surreal.

As I left the restroom, I headed to the marquee to grab a drink. The room was empty save for me and two other people who were walking together, deep in conversation. I headed over to where the drinks were and realised that one of them was Jeff Munson – Paisley Park's ex-Art Director – and a guest speaker on the 'Prince Interactive' panel earlier. I said "Hello," and he said "Hi," and he asked if I was having a good day. I said that it had surpassed my wildest expectations and he laughed and said, "Well, that's Paisley Park for you."

I told him he was enormously lucky to have worked here and to have known Prince, and he was extremely gracious in his response. He introduced me to his friend, and we chatted for a minute or two longer before I felt I should get back to the show.

I shook Jeff's hand and he said, "Great to meet you, Stuart."

I headed back in to meet Jonathan and Ben. It wasn't long before Parliament-Funkadelic's riotous set ended and the house lights came up. Damaris Lewis was back on the stage. She told us that tomorrow would be just as incredible as today had been. She repeated her mantra, "Listen. Learn. Teach. Love." As she left the stage, Joel Weinshanker appeared briefly and thanked us for our attendance. The doors were opened wide as the audience departed the Soundstage. It took a good ten minutes before we were able to get through the packed exit. I noted that the merchandise stall was now closed. It had easily been one of the most incredible days of my life and we headed back to the marquee, pausing to have our cell phones unlocked before stepping out into the bright sunlight once more.

Suddenly, Joel Weinshanker was standing right there, greeting everyone as they left. He shook my hand warmly, and thanked me for coming. He told us he would see us again tomorrow and I smiled and thanked him back for this wonderful experience, before we headed back to the front of Paisley Park. I have to confess that by this point in the day, nothing surprised me anymore. As we stood in the parking lot at the front of Prince's house, I looked at the building. It was unfamiliar to me no more. I felt closer to Prince than I had ever felt before, and my heart soared.

We walked towards the gates that lead out onto Audubon Road, and I called Joanne – our cab driver – who picked up in a heartbeat.

"Is that you, Stuart?" she asked before I could speak.

"Yes, it's me," I said. "Can you come collect us please, Joanne?"

Joanne told me she'd be five minutes. She arrived in less than three. She had brought a female friend with her, "Just to meet you guys."

Jonathan, Ben, and I laughed and climbed into the taxi which took us back to our hotel at West 78th Street. Joanne dropped us at the door and reminded me to call her if I ever needed a ride. I thanked her, and told her I'd do that. Maybe one day I might.

We headed to the dining area of the hotel and got some drinks, and I began talking to a lady who was nearby. She introduced herself and I invited Monica to join our table. Monica asked if we were Prince *fam*, and I told her that we were, and that morning we'd been to Paisley Park for the first time. We chatted for a while, swapping stories about growing up as followers of Prince's music, and she laughed as she told us about her father's disdain at her sister's infatuation with Minneapolis' favourite son, and how she had hidden the infamous shower poster from the *Controversy* album on the back of her bedroom door from him.

Monica then dropped a bombshell that stopped the conversation dead. She handed me her business card.

"I manage Shelby J from the NPG," she said. "We're staying at this hotel."

Having spent more than a decade as a member of the New Power Generation, with credits including lead vocals on the second single 'Chelsea Rodgers' – from Prince's 2007 album *Planet Earth* – and performing at the now-legendary Super Bowl XLI halftime show in Miami that year, Shelby Johnson has musical chops in abundance.

A native of Greensboro North Carolina, Shelby was born to sing. As a youngster, her mother led the choir in their local church, and Shelby enjoyed the opportunity this afforded her to perform from a young age. As she grew up, Shelby would sing in restaurants, bars, anywhere in fact, that would give her an audience. She paid her dues on the road and some nights it was tough. Playing to tiny audiences and earning next to nothing might have broken a less-determined soul, but not Shelby J, as she is known onstage. She kept at it with dogged determination, honing her craft – and in the process – building formidable performance skills. An R&B singer possessed with exceptional vocal ability, it was only a matter of time before the right opportunity came along.

Shelby got her first break in 1992, when she joined a local jazz trio named In the Black, and she spent some time performing on cruise ships with the band before heading to New York, where her career took off in earnest. Working as a touring vocalist, she performed with Santana, Mary J Blige, and D'Angelo amongst others.

In the fall of 2006, she got a call from Larry Graham of Sly and the Family Stone. Larry was now the bassist with Prince's band, and he asked her if she'd like to perform at the 3121 club in Las Vegas. She flew out to Vegas and prepared for the show. That night – not realising that Prince was in attendance – Shelby – under the impression that she was filling in for a sick vocalist and would be on the way home the following day – performed like the consummate professional. Mid-number – to her surprise – she turned to see Prince onstage singing with her. Her fate was sealed, and realising she'd just been in an audition of sorts – albeit one that was more a baptism of fire – she was in. Prince immediately asked her to join his band.

Shelby was working with fellow North Carolina musician and songwriter Anthony Hamilton at the time, and she called him to tell him that she was joining Prince. She was nervous about Anthony's reaction but he was fine, even joking that he'd leave his own band to join Prince. From there, her ascendancy was assured.

A striking woman, Shelby's captivating smile ranks as one of the most infectious I've ever seen, and her radiant personality warmed the entire room. Shelby fronted her own band, Black Gypsy, and was an astute businesswoman with her own company which specialised in providing positive messages for youngsters through music, books, and performance. Ever striving for artistic success, she hoped to break into TV and movie roles, as well as Broadway performance.

Monica asked us what our plans were later. I told her that we weren't sure. She said that Shelby was performing at the Dakota Jazz Club that evening, and I told her that we were aware of this, but we didn't have tickets. She asked us to go and we agreed to, and then Monica was off, taking calls. After she left, I looked at her card. It was black and purple. I placed it in my wallet as a memento.

Back in the UK in June of 2016 – after I had decided that I would be making the trip to Minneapolis – a few Prince *fam* I knew had toyed with the notion of organising a group visit to Prince's hometown. I was going regardless of whether this would happen or not, but the idea of travelling with a plane full of British *fam* had genuinely appealed to me. We talked excitedly about chartering a plane if we could get enough people to attend. For the idea to fly – literally – we needed two hundred people to get on board. Sadly, the planned visit *en masse* to Minneapolis fizzled out as these things are often prone to do. One of the people involved, Mark – who had started a group on social media for the planned group event – kept in touch with me afterward and said he would definitely be making the journey to Paisley Park in April too.

Born in Birmingham in 1969, Mark now lived in Tamworth with this wife and three children, working as an Outdoor Industry Consultant. Raised on a childhood diet of Miles Davis and Santana, it was perhaps inevitable that he would find Prince, as both artists were a huge influence on Prince's music. Mark had seen Prince live even more times than I had, and once kissed him on the shoulder in Las Vegas as Prince walked past. In his teens he once snuck out of the house and hitchhiked to Paris to see Prince. He'd been an avid supporter of Aston Villa football club his entire life. He first heard Prince at a school disco in 1982 when the DJ played '1999' and a week later Mark saw the promo video. He was instantly hooked. Years later, Mark sang '1999' at his wedding. He rates his performance – somewhat modestly – as a six out of ten. Like me, he ranks 1987's *Sign o' the Times* album as Prince's best work.

Over the year since Prince's passing, Mark and I had become

firm friends, sharing anecdotes and stories about our hero. Although we had never met in person, we felt a kinship over our shared love of Prince's work, and Mark told me that he was looking forward to meeting me for the first time in Chanhassen. Sadly, he was unable to attend the opening day of *Celebration 2017* as it was his daughter's birthday the day before – an important occasion that he understandably couldn't miss – and his flight was scheduled to land in Minnesota around the moment I was watching George Clinton and P-Funk perform at Paisley Park. Mark was staying at our hotel for a few days before spending the rest of his time in Minneapolis in accommodation Downtown.

Mark had messaged me to say that he was in Minneapolis-Saint Paul airport and would be at the hotel an hour from now. I went up to my room, dumped my bags, and freshened up before catching up with social media.

I quickly made some notes about the day's events. After a time, Mark messaged again to say he was in his room and I said I'd meet him downstairs when he was ready. I sat in the lobby and presently he came down the stairs. We hugged and sat down to talk.

Usually when you meet someone for the first time, the conversation can be a little stilted, but it didn't happen with us. We chatted away like we'd met a thousand times, and he asked how the first day of *Celebration 2017* had been, and what Paisley Park had been like. He sat wide-eyed as I told him about the things I had seen and the people I had met. He said that he was excited about what was to come. I told him that before we were back at Paisley Park the following day at 5.00pm, we had another list of sites to visit that had associations with Prince. I said he was more than welcome to come along and he enthusiastically agreed to do so. I then informed Mark that we would be going to the Dakota Jazz Club to see Shelby J perform that night. Mark had already booked a ticket, so was happy that we would be going too, and he offered to drive us to the show.

Jonathan and Ben came down from their rooms and I introduced them to Mark and we agreed to go for dinner at

Chuck Wagon Charlie's again to see our old friend Shane. Before we headed out to the bar, Mark laughed and said, "Come and see the car I've got."

We walked outside to the hotel parking lot and Mark pointed to his hire car, a maroon 4.6 litre Ford Mustang convertible. He started it up and we listened to the engine's throaty growl. As he opened the door, the side view mirror projected an illuminated silhouette of a galloping Mustang pony onto the floor alongside the car.

"Puddle lights," he grinned.

We laughed and I inspected the inside of the American car. I had never seen so much neon lighting inside an automobile. It looked like a spaceship.

We walked the short distance to Shane's bar and went inside. Like the last time, it was quiet and Shane was standing behind the bar watching a game on TV with a few locals. Without being asked, he fixed us some drinks before bringing us some menus.

"How is the trip going, guys?" he enquired. "Seen much Prince stuff?"

We talked to him enthusiastically about the events that had happened and he sat and listened, nodding approvingly. While the others ordered a round of burgers and chicken wings with a variety of dressings, I opted for a salad.

Shane laughed and said, "Going for the healthy option, eh? Good choice. It is – of course – huge."

We finished our meals at 9.00pm and decided to drive Downtown to the Dakota. Shelby's show at the club was due to start around 10.30pm so we got in the Mustang. Mark put the address into the GPS on his phone and we set off. Along the way, we took a multitude of wrong turns. Mark's reactions to these were hilarious. He cursed and shouted at other drivers and at the road, and we all laughed a lot.

"I'm under way too much pressure with strangers in the car!" he joked.

We played Prince tunes loudly and sang along with gusto.

Driving around foreign cities is always an exhilarating experience – particularly at night – and this short forty minute drive under neon lights in Prince's home town while listening to his music felt magical. There was nowhere else on Earth I wanted to be right then.

We arrived at the Dakota Jazz Club at 1010 Nicollet Mall, and Mark parked the car on the roadside opposite Target Plaza on South 10th Street. We got out, and for a minute he worried that the car might get a ticket – or even get towed – and we read the confusing parking signs. After deciding it was safe to leave the car there, we walked across the street to the Dakota. We got to the welcome desk and to my relief our names were on the list. Mark was seated on the ground floor while Jonathan, Ben, and I were on the first floor balcony in front of the stage. We were shown to our seats and walked right past Prince's table. Our tables were just feet away from the spot he sat at a few days before his passing. The card was on his table, and fresh flowers were placed there.

The table I was allocated was already occupied. I sat down, and introduced myself to the lady sitting there. Her name was Natasha. After ordering some drinks from our server, we began talking and Natasha told me that she was born in Chicago, and now lived in Florida. She thought I was Scottish. I told her she wasn't the first person on this trip to say that, and she laughed. She was there for the anniversary weekend but was not going to *Celebration 2017*, instead preferring to leave a note on the fence at Paisley Park much like I had originally intended to do. We talked for a while about Prince – and about ourselves – before the lights went down, and the show began.

A mesmerising performer, Shelby was incredible onstage. Her voice is wonderful and she sang songs from her soulful forthcoming album, *10*, which was out later that week. Between numbers she talked about Prince a lot – and how he was her mentor – and she said that we were united in our love for him. She pointed to his table, and told us that others from his bands were there, including the NPG's Liv Warfield and Marva King, and members of 3rdeyegirl. Donna Grantis – the guitarist with Prince's last band – acknowledged this and waved to everyone from her table to the right of the stage. A cheer went up when the audience spotted her.

During Shelby's performance, all three joined her onstage for different numbers, and Donna performed a blistering guitar solo at one point. Shelby was also accompanied onstage for one song by a grey-haired woman from the audience called Doris who, after kissing the entire band – Shelby included – grabbed a tambourine and did the most incredible frenzied James Brown-style dancing while banging the instrument enthusiastically. Shelby was amazed and said that she would pay Doris' bill for the night, lightheartedly saying, "Doris isn't paying for her liquor or her parmesan grits."

Everyone went wild.

At several points during the show, Shelby looked up to us on the balcony, winking and smiling. It had been ten years since I first saw her perform in London with Prince, and I felt blessed to have this opportunity to see her sing again.

At the climax of the show, Shelby performed a trio of Prince's numbers and during a sensational rendition of 'I Wanna Be Your Lover' from his 1979 album *Prince*, she began a chant of "We love you, Prince."

The audience seized the opportunity and as we sang along, everyone was on their feet dancing. Natasha and I danced and hugged and for a few minutes the room was lost to the glorious chant. It was a hugely emotional moment on which to end the night and it was a perfect tribute to Prince.

As I was thinking that the night couldn't get any better, Shelby's manager Monica came over. She was jubilant and in the middle of this amazing evening in a packed club, I couldn't believe she'd taken the trouble to find me. She thanked me for coming. I thanked her for inviting us, telling her we'd had an incredible night.

Monica smiled and handed me something.

I looked at it and it was a CD-R of Shelby's new album.

It wasn't out for another week, but Monica told me that Shelby had made a very small number of these by hand. The customised case was embellished with stick-on jewels. I was touched that she had given it to me and I thanked her for it and then she was off again, clearly a lady in huge demand this evening.

I said goodbye to Natasha, telling her to enjoy the rest of her time in Minneapolis. Me, Jonathan and Ben headed down the stairs to meet up with Mark who had enjoyed the show up-close in front of the stage. We headed to the right of the stage and the exit. Suddenly there was a scramble and we found ourselves standing next to Donna Grantis from 3rdeyegirl. She graciously posed for photos with each of us, and we walked outside into the cool Minneapolis night, ecstatic to have been at the Dakota Jazz Club on such a special evening.

We headed back to the hotel. On the drive back, we discussed the arrangements for tomorrow. We were at Paisley Park from 5.00pm until 10.00pm, so had the day to visit the rest of the places on my list. We played some deep cuts from Prince's back catalogue and I suggested 'Calhoun Square' from the 1998 compilation *Crystal Ball*. The song is named after a place in Uptown Minneapolis that we would be visiting in the morning, so it felt like an appropriate choice. As the songs played and we drove the quiet streets back to beautiful Chanhassen, I reflected on how amazing this trip had been. I'd hoped it would be a once in a lifetime experience and with another four days ahead of us it had already turned out to be just that. Tired and happy, we got back to our rooms around 3.00am and I called my wife, but she didn't answer. I texted her to say I was safe in my room and I immediately drifted off to sleep, waking a few hours later.

Calhoun Square in Uptown.

The gates of Prince's 'Purple House' on Kiowa Trail.

Me outside Prince's home, Paisley Park.

The *Purple Rain* house on Snelling Avenue South.

Onstage at First Avenue. *Purple Rain* was recorded on this very spot.

915 Logan Avenue North. Prince lived at this address until he was eight.

The Sing A Song Of Uptown mural.

Jonathan and Ben at South 7th Street.
Our first morning in Minneapolis.

5708 Stevens Avenue South.
The site of the original Moon Sound Studio.

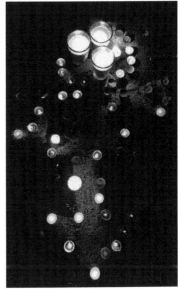

2201 5th Avenue South.
Prince's first home.

Love symbol candles
at the midnight vigil.

Me and the wonderful Shelby J.

Me onstage at The Capri Theater.

2620 North 8th Avenue.

Me and Mark sitting front row at the Capri.

Me at First Avenue.

Prince's star outside First Avenue.

Prince Rogers Nelson 1958-2016.

FRIDAY

We convened in the breakfast area of the hotel early the next morning and over food we talked about the day ahead. That evening at Paisley Park we would be seeing Prince's most famous backing band – The Revolution – both in conversation and performance. We were excited at the prospect, and it felt quite apt to be seeing them on this date. It was April 21, 2017. The first anniversary of Prince's passing. I said that we'd have to pick up the Minneapolis Star Tribune – the city's newspaper – today as it would inevitably be full of articles to commemorate Prince. I messaged my wife, asking her to pick up the papers for me back in the UK too. She replied a few hours later that she'd done this for me. Mark offered to drive today, and it was beautiful outside. The Mustang was a convertible, and the thought of driving around Minneapolis on a sunny day with the roof down was very appealing, so I accepted his kind offer and we headed out. It was early and we had a lot to fit in.

Uptown – a commercial quarter located a mile south-west of Downtown Minneapolis – is a bustling commercial district that has undergone gentrification in recent years. Named after the old Lagoon Theater, which burnt down in 1939 and was replaced by the Uptown Theater, the district proved to be a popular location for local artists and musicians, and as well as being a cultural hub, many clubs and bars are now situated there. Uptown has become a desirable residential location offering amenities that provide an attractive alternative to the more hectic Downtown. In 1980, Prince released *Dirty Mind*, his brilliant third studio album which included the track 'Uptown'; a paean to the district. Within a few years of Prince's song, a shopping mall named Calhoun Square was built on the corner of West Lake Street and Hennepin Avenue, and it is this building that is commemorated in the song of the same name. 'Calhoun Square' remained unreleased in Prince's vault from its recording in 1993 until its inclusion on the *Crystal Ball* triple album, released five years later in 1998. Prince clearly loved the area and in the mid-'90s, he opened the New Power Generation retail store on West Lake Street. Sadly, the store is now closed, but the business that opened in the unit afterward – Go Home Furnishings – kept the purple front door for many years in honour of the building's former tenant.

From our hotel it was approximately twenty miles to Calhoun Square in Uptown, and we drove east from Chanhassen along Minnesota State Highway 5, passing through the suburb of Eden Prairie – home to former NPG drummer Michael Bland aka Michael B – before joining Route 212, and heading north on Minnesota State Highway 100 at Edina. Paul Peterson, one time member of Prince protégés The Time and The Family, resided in this small city. Taking Excelsior Boulevard and heading north-east, we joined West Lake Street. Heading east, we crossed the bridge between Lake Calhoun and Lake of the Isles and approached Uptown. We continued along West Lake Street and we spotted our destination ahead, parking the car on Irving Avenue South on our right. It was 8.30am.

Walking easterly along West Lake Street, we passed Calhoun Beach Framing and the Lake and Irving Restaurant and Bar. Crossing Humboldt Avenue South, we went by the huge Sons of Norway building on our right before crossing Holmes Avenue, and there on the right was Calhoun Square. It's a huge building with a fantastic sign on the roof which reminded me a little of the Statue of Liberty's crown. We took photos of each other outside this building immortalised in song by Prince, and looking across the street we spotted the Uptown Theater at the intersection of

Hennepin Avenue and Lagoon Avenue. The theatre was now an art-house cinema mostly showing independent and foreign language films, and the beautiful art deco building featured a sixty foot high tower with the word 'Uptown' on it on three sides. We spent a time simply walking around and soaking up the cool ambience of this desirable area of Minneapolis.

As we walked back along the route we came, we stumbled across a fabulous multi-coloured mural at the corner of Lyndale Avenue and West Lake Street. It is known as the *Sing a Song of Uptown* mural. Completed in 2016 by Greta McLain, this stunning work of art features blocks of colour and surreal imagery. Facing a small narrow alley, it covered the entire northwest facade of the Rainbow House building. We were astounded at our unintentional find and took lots of photos as people entered and exited the building before we headed back to the car. From parking the car to setting off again, I had the tune to 'Calhoun Square' playing in my head virtually the entire time we were in Uptown. Stopping at a gas station, I picked up a handful of copies of the Minneapolis Star Tribune. Prince was all over it. Throwing them in the trunk, we left Uptown and headed east a mile and a half on West 31st Street into the Central neighbourhood before turning right. Four blocks down on the right was the site of Prince's old High School at 3416 4th Avenue South.

Minneapolis Central High School was no longer there. Demolished after closing in 1982, the Richard R Green Central Elementary School now occupied the site where Prince graduated in 1976. The current building had a huge mural on one side and we stopped to take pictures of the site where the schoolyard Prince hung out in as a youth once stood.

From 4th Avenue South we drove south just two blocks to our next stop. Turning west onto East 38th Street – just past the offices of the Minnesota Spokesman-Recorder – we stopped outside the Sabathani Community Center. This was the site of Prince's former middle school, Bryant Junior High. It was at this school that Prince took a keen interest in basketball, and photos of him wearing his vest and shorts in the early '70s exist online. Sadly, none of Prince's schools exist anymore. We took photos of the site and moved on to the final education centre associated with Prince on our trip.

The site of the old John Hay Elementary School lay at the intersection of North Oak Park Avenue and Penn Avenue North in North Minneapolis. It was approximately eight miles from where we were. Travelling twenty five blocks east on East 38th Street, we headed north on 23rd Avenue South before joining Hiawatha Avenue. Taking the I-94 West, we continued until turning north onto Lyndale Avenue South and passing the stunning Basilica of Saint Mary. Opened in 1907, this neoclassical Roman Catholic Church is the earliest example in the United States. As we passed it, Jonathan took photos. Joining East Lyndale Avenue North, we took a left onto Olson Memorial Highway. Travelling west and passing the turn for North Newton Avenue where we met Reese Philips – Prince's brother-in-law – I remarked that we were here a few days ago.

Taking a right onto Penn Avenue North, our destination was two blocks ahead of us, but Mark took a left turn a block early onto North 8th Avenue. Realising our mistake, he drove two blocks and turned right at Queen Avenue North. Emerging at Oak Park Avenue North, he turned right and after a block we arrived at the site of Prince's old Elementary School. It was just an empty patch of fenced off ground, adjacent to the Lincoln Community School. As we took photos, I noted that sadly the site was in need of repair. An abandoned children's play area stood forlornly in the centre of the site. Our next stop was the first of three houses we were visiting today that Prince lived in as a child.

Starting the car, Mark drove us east along Oak Park Avenue North for eight blocks. Turning right onto Logan Avenue North, the residence we were looking for was number 915. It was the fourth house on the right. Prince's parents moved here on New Year's Eve 1958 from his first home at 2201 5th Avenue South –

the house near the Electric Fetus record store – when he was still a baby. Prince lived here until the age of seven.

We pulled up outside the property and saw that a Hispanic family were busy at the house next door. There was a removal truck parked outside and it appeared that someone was possibly moving in or moving out. As we took pictures of each other – and the house – one of them came over to us and asked why we were interested in it.

Mark told him that Prince lived on this spot as a child.

"*The* Prince?" he asked, incredulously.

Mark confirmed that he was correct and the man walked back to his family, relaying the information that Mark had just given him.

Next, a girl came over and asked if it is true that Prince lived next door to her house. I told her it was, and I asked her how long her family had lived there.

She said, "Maybe ten years!" and walked back to her family, laughing.

Sadly, the small blue weatherboard house at 915 Logan Avenue North was not the actual house that Prince lived in. The original home was torn down and replaced with the one that now stands on its spot in 1995. As part of the Prince story though, this was still an important site. It was likely to be the spot where he started an interest in music, and it was probable that the young musical prodigy learned to play the piano here, aged just seven years old.

We drove to the end of the block and turned right onto North 8th Avenue, a street we were on a little earlier. Heading west for sixteen blocks, we arrived at number 2620 on the right where a yellow single storey house with a double garage stood on the intersection with Upton Avenue North. Prince lived here from 1965. Around this time, his parent's marriage began to deteriorate and a few years later – most likely 1969 – John L Nelson moved out, returning to Logan Avenue North – which he had shrewdly kept and rented out – leaving his children at this address with their mother. In 1970, Mattie married Hayward Baker – father of Prince's half-brother Omarr – and the family continued to live here. When Prince's father left, he didn't take his piano with him, which afforded the youngster more opportunity to play. Prince apparently wrote his first song – 'Funk Machine' – at this address. I marvelled at the fact that the career I have followed so keenly for most of my life began right here. We took photos of each other standing outside the house. While we were at this property, a thought suddenly occurred to me regarding the homes that Prince lived in as a child. They all appeared to be unoccupied. While we were at this address, Mark commented that the locations we had visited should be put together in an official tour, and joked that I should be employed as the tour guide.

We turned right onto Upton Avenue North, and right again at the end of the block, back onto Oak Park Avenue North. Driving five blocks, we turned left onto a pretty street. A block and a half up on the right side was the childhood home of André Anderson – later André Cymone – at 1244 Russell Avenue North. After Prince's father threw him out of the house on Newton Avenue North – where we met Reese Phillips – he was taken in by Bernadette Anderson, André's mother. At this house, the two boys practised music incessantly in the basement where Prince slept, and it is likely that the famous sound of Minneapolis was born here.

As we stood outside the immaculate property – it had arched windows and was situated up a small grassy embankment – a woman passerby asked us who had lived there. We told her and she said she was a huge Prince *fam* and we chatted for a few minutes. To my amusement, I realised as we talked that she looked remarkably like a female Dez Dickerson, a former bandmate of Prince's. The wrought-iron handrail at the concrete steps leading up to the house had purple ribbon wrapped around it, and the house was surrounded by perfectly manicured conifers. The white front door had a sunrise on it. The property reminded me of a small church. Next door to André's house – at 1248 Russell Avenue – was the old childhood home of Terry Jackson, who was also a band-mate of Prince and André in their first band, Grand Central. A young Morris Day – later the front man for The Time

– was their drummer. Another beautifully-kept residence, it was also the site of many band auditions and rehearsals which were instrumental in the young Prince's early musical forays.

From there, we drove to the end of the street – past Terry Jackson's house – and turned right onto Plymouth Avenue North. A mile north, we took a right onto 26th Avenue North, and then right again onto Logan Avenue North, parking the Mustang just before the intersection with West Broadway Avenue. We could see our next destination across the busy street.

The Capri Theater at 2027 West Broadway Avenue was built in 1927. It seats just five hundred patrons, and on January 5th and 6th 1979 Prince performed his very first solo shows here as a signed artist. Although he had been picked up by Warner Brothers a few years earlier and had released his first album *For You* in 1978, it wasn't until this time that Prince formed a band and finally played live. The shows – which were priced at four dollars a ticket – were attended by label executives who were there to gauge whether the young musician was ready to venture further afield. The shows were billed as benefit performances and the revenue raised from ticket sales went back to the Capri. Amongst the songs Prince performed at these shows were the title track from his debut LP, 'Soft and Wet', and 'Just As Long As We're Together', a song he had originally recorded live in real-time in the studio for executives when auditioning for the label.

As we stood outside the Capri taking photos, another party of Prince *fam* arrived. I tried the door to the theatre, but it was closed. Mark looked into the building before turning to me and saying, "There are pictures of Prince on the wall."

I peered through the glass, and there in the lobby were framed black and white photographs from the shows that had taken place inside this modest building all those years ago. As I looked at them, Mark went around to the west side of the building and spotted a man inside the Capri, who was dressed in overalls and who was halfway up a ladder fitting a new light fixture. Mark tapped on the glass and asked if the guy inside could open up the theatre for us to have a quick look around. The man motioned back that he wasn't able to open the doors and didn't have a key. Mark, pushing his luck somewhat – he's an insistent type but charming with it – asked him to ring the manager of the Capri, and the guy laughed and asked us to give him a few minutes.

Presently, the Director of the Capri – a gentleman named James Scott – arrived and we explained politely that we had travelled from the UK and asked if it was possible for him to allow us inside his historic little theatre.

"I suppose I'd better if you've come all this way!" he joked, and unlocked the front door of the red brick and orange-painted building.

We thanked him and walked in, heading straight to the photos hanging on the walls. The amazing pictures – taken by Greg Helgeson – showed Prince and his band sporting thigh-high legwarmers and leopard-print clothes, and gave an indication of what would come later in Prince's career. His androgynous persona and outrageous sexual image come through in the photos, even at this early stage.

The doors to the auditorium inside the Capri were closed, and – taking a turn to push my luck – I asked James if we could see the performance area.

He said, "Sure," and opened the doors to the room where the photos were taken. The auditorium was small and the walls facing the stage were painted with large black and red squares. Two rows of red seats faced the stage. We asked James if we could sit in them and he said we could so we took the opportunity to take photos of each other on the front row. I pictured Prince and his band leaping around the small stage. James – sensing our excitement – asked us if we would like to get up on the spot where the band had performed. We didn't need asking twice, and were on the stage in seconds. I asked James if the room had changed much since 1979, and he said that it was largely the same. We goofed around on the stage for a few minutes, and Mark took a great photo of me doing a Prince-style leap with my arms and legs outstretched, capturing me mid-air. I was thrilled to be allowed on the stage at the Capri and I spent a long time taking photos of everything, including the lighting and sound console at the back of the auditorium.

We went back into the lobby and James told us that the Capri was currently in the middle of refurbishment, having been granted funds from the government. We wrote messages in the visitor's book and I took the opportunity to use the restroom before we left, and we thanked James for giving us the opportunity to see this wonderful – and hugely important – piece of Prince's history. He said he was pleased to help, and we walked back to the car in the beautiful sunshine, thoroughly elated.

Before we got to it, a huge truck drove toward us as we crossed the street, and Mark put his fist up and pulled it down sharply in the universal gesture to indicate to the driver to blow his air horn which – to our delight – he did. Laughing, we ran to the car and putting the roof down – and Prince's 1978 *For You* album on the stereo – we set off to our next destination.

The Cozy Bar and Lounge was originally located at 522 Plymouth Avenue, just north of Downtown West. Owned by James T 'Jimmie' Fuller, Sr, the bar was torn down sometime around 1977 to make way for the I-94 Freeway after Fuller Sr sold it to Minnesota's Department of Transport. The Cozy Bar was one of the few black-owned bars in Minneapolis and was an early venue for Prince's band, Grand Central.

We travelled east along West Broadway Avenue. Passing O'Reilly's Auto Parts and Minneapolis Public Schools, we continued east for sixteen blocks. Just after the Taco Bell, the road traversed the busy I-94. It was at this spot that Cozy's once stood. As we passed the site we estimated the bar to have stood on, we raised our hands up in the open top Mustang and waved to nobody in particular as confirmation to ourselves that we had located the spot. Some people waved back and we laughed. Jonathan grabbed some photos of the area from the back seat of the car.

Unfortunately, our haste in leaving the Capri was such that I got the order of our destinations wrong, and as we passed over the Mississippi River, I consulted my notes and discovered that we were around five miles in the wrong direction.

Across the river, Mark turned the car westward and we travelled back the way we had just come. Turning left onto Girard Avenue North at the Shiloh Temple, we took our first right onto Golden Valley Road before taking Toledo Avenue North as far as Thotland Road, and then heading south on Lilac Drive North and crossing Highway 55 via the Olsen Highway Service Road. Rejoining Lilac Drive North, we turned left onto Turners Crossroad North and then right onto Glenwood Avenue just near to the Golden Valley Lutheran Church. Our destination was a short way along Glenwood and on the left.

115 King Creek Road was an immaculately kept half-million dollar property in a beautiful suburb of Minneapolis where Prince's mother, Mattie, had lived with his stepfather, Hayward. As we drove onto the street, a security guard – clearly employed to keep out unwanted visitors – watched us keenly before getting into a car and leaving. To our delight, the house opposite 115 King Creek Road had an automobile reversing out of the drive. The car looked to be a white '60s Ford Thunderbird convertible or similar, and it was almost identical to the one Prince drives in the 1986 movie *Under the Cherry Moon*. The driver stopped alongside our Mustang and grinned, giving us a thumbs-up as we took pictures of this amazing car in front of the house we were there to see. We wondered aloud if the owner had chosen it because of the Prince connection to the house on his street.

Our next stop had huge importance in Prince's story. It was the little house with a basement studio where he recorded the 1976 demos that would ultimately lead to the Minneapolis wunderkind securing his first recording contract.

This was our penultimate destination before our second day at *Celebration 2017* in Paisley Park which was due to begin at 5.00pm later that afternoon. On the ten mile drive to it, we reflected on the day we'd had. It was still early – around 11.30am – and Mark was astounded by the things we'd already seen this morning and expressed sadness at not having been here the previous two days, but he was excited about seeing Prince's home later. As we headed east on I-394, we played Prince on the stereo, and skirting the Loring Park neighbourhood, we spotted the Basilica of Saint Mary once more.

Joining Dunwoody Boulevard, we turned right and headed south on Lyndale Avenue South before turning the Mustang eastward on West Franklin Avenue and then south on Blaisdell Avenue. Crossing West Lake Street – where Calhoun Square, our first stop this morning was – we joined the I-35W heading south before passing the neighbourhoods of Regina, Field, and Tangletown. We then merged with Stevens Avenue, and the South Minneapolis address we were heading to.

5708 Stevens Avenue South was a tidy little house whose modest appearance belied its importance in the development of Prince's early career as a fledgling recording artist. It was here in 1976 – while Prince was still at Central High School – that he began an association with a white Englishman named Chris Moon who would prove pivotal in providing the young musician with the skills necessary to court major record companies. Chris – a talented sound engineer – owned a small studio named Moon Sound in the basement of the property we were at.

Prince and his band, Champagne, visited Stevens Avenue to record in the basement and Chris instantly recognised that Prince stood out. He offered the talented young musician free studio time with tuition in multi-track recording. In exchange, Chris – a budding song-smith – requested the opportunity for the two to work together on poems and lyrics he had written. Prince agreed and was soon given his own key to the studio, thus enabling him to access instruments and equipment with ease at weekends and after school. Shortly after their alliance began, Prince left Champagne, deciding that his future path to fame and fortune was as a solo musician. He learned quickly how to use the studio and as his skills as a musician developed, it soon became apparent that it was time to put together some recordings with a view to approaching record labels.

Songs the pair worked on around this time included 'My Love Is Forever' and 'Soft and Wet', a number they co-wrote which later became Prince's first single in June 1978. Ultimately, the demo tape the two young men produced in 1976 failed to get Prince the record deal he desired, but his association with Chris Moon led directly to Prince – aged just seventeen – signing a management contract with local businessman Owen Husney. The songs from Prince's Moon Sound demo were re-recorded and packaged in an attractive press kit which was distributed to prospective labels, and interest in this young musician – billed as the new Stevie Wonder – began in earnest.

The street was deserted, and we stood outside the property where Prince spent countless hours as a young boy, developing his chops. I remarked that the residence was tiny, and looking in the window it appeared to be unoccupied. The exterior of the wooden house was painted white, and the window frames were forest green. We took photos of each other in front of the property, and out of the corner of my eye I spotted something unusual. On the inside of the window sill above the house number to the right of the front door, was a little oval plastic sign. It was about eight inches long by two inches high and it was just sitting there, balancing against the glass. It was purple.

I stared at the words on the sign. *Welcome to Moon Sound. Established 1974.* For a second I was incredulous. How long had this sign been here? Who put it there? As I asked myself these questions, I shouted excitedly to Jonathan, Ben, and Mark, and they walked over. They looked at the sign in disbelief and we took photos of each other with it. After a short time spent relaxing and taking photos at the house on Stevens Avenue South – during which time we played 'Soft and Wet' on the car stereo in homage to the little studio that once stood on this spot – we decided to move on to the final place we planned to visit today before making our way to Paisley Park and the incredible events that were about to unfold there.

In the movie *Purple Rain*, Prince's character 'The Kid' takes his female lead, Apollonia, to Lake Minnetonka – meaning 'Great Water' – where when told that she must "Purify herself in Lake Minnetonka", she strips naked and jumps into the freezing water to prove her determination to become a star under his tutelage. The scene has become famous for the line Prince utters as the dripping wet Apollonia scrambles up the bank from the water. As she gathers her clothes, he delivers the killer blow, "That ain't Lake Minnetonka."

The actual location used for the shooting of this scene has always been in some dispute, but as we were in Minnesota – and figuring that this might be our only chance to come here – we decided to drive to the lake anyway, regardless of whether it was the true spot where Apollonia takes a dip or not.

We headed west from Moon Sound on Stevens Avenue, and drove through the city of Minnetonka in Hennepin County. Continuing eastward on MN-7, we skirted Excelsior and passed Shorewood, following Smithtown Road until we saw a sign for Howard's Point Marina. Turning right, we drove slowly along Howard's Point Road taking in the homes around us on both sides.

The properties here were stunning and many overlooked the water that seemed to be constantly within our sight. Property prices in this part of Minneapolis run to several millions of dollars. Residents mowed their lawns and pruned immaculate shrubbery as we passed them. We stopped and chatted for a moment to a lady who was tending her garden. Mark asked about the tall thin poles that ran the perimeter of the drive, from the house to the road. Each had a brightly coloured loop at the top.

"They're to find the way when it snows," she said. "It can get pretty deep here."

We told her that we thought the railroad trestle scene in *Purple Rain* had been shot around Howard's Point Road, and we enquired whether she knew where it might be located. She informed us that there were no old rail bridges around this area, so feeling a little deflated at not finding our intended spot we made the most of it and used the opportunity to enjoy driving around this beautiful lake-filled area for a while.

After an hour of leisurely travel around Minnetonka, Lake Virginia, and Schutz Lake, we headed south on Rolling Acres Road before taking a right and travelling past Minnesota Landscape Arboretum. We followed Arboretum Boulevard, and on the way back to Chanhassen we stopped at a fast food restaurant on Century Boulevard. In need of refreshments, Mark parked the car and we headed inside.

As we ate, construction workers looked at us quizzically, probably wondering what these four British men - three of whom had accents that no doubt sounded vaguely Scottish – were doing there at two o'clock on this unfeasibly hot Friday afternoon in April.

Arriving back at the hotel on West 78th Street a little while later, Jonathan, Ben and I decided to walk the short distance to Target to purchase some candles. As this was the anniversary of Prince's passing, a vigil was taking place at the Riley Creek underpass that ran underneath Highway 5.

This tunnel was located right outside Paisley Park and was accessed by a footpath running alongside the front fence. I chose a large ten dollar purple candle that smelled of lavender. We got back to our rooms and I freshened up and called my wife to tell her about my day. I quickly sent her the pictures I had taken over the past two days, and ensuring she had received them all, I cleared my phone's cache. Heading down to the lobby at 4.00pm, I met up with my companions and we headed out to Paisley Park, choosing to go in Mark's car as it was still a warm afternoon.

As we crawled down Audubon Road alongside the Paisley Park complex, there were Prince *fam* everywhere, and as we passed them – playing his tunes with the hood down – they cheered and waved at us appreciatively. It was a glorious day and there wasn't a cloud in the beautiful blue sky. Everyone was in a buoyant mood. We parked the car fifty feet up Park Road – the street behind

Paisley Park – leaving the Mustang right near the Chanhassen Lakes Business Park sign.

This was Mark's first time inside Paisley Park and I could tell that he was excitably nervous. We walked briskly back along Audubon Road, and reaching the gate to Prince's home, we stopped to take pictures of each other leaning on the wooden address sign that stood outside the entrance. Continuing past the gates towards Highway 5, we turned right at the fence and followed the path eastward along the front of the complex and down to the Riley Creek underpass.

The perimeter railing in front of Paisley Park had flowers and dozens of notes tied to it, and little purple padlocks – each engraved with a Prince lyric – slowly rusting as they hung on the fence. Placed there by grieving *fam* in the days after we lost him, they were a poignant reminder of that dreadful day exactly a year ago. The entire length of the four hundred foot long path at our feet was awash with chalked messages. There were *hundreds* of them. Some mourned his passing, others quoted lyrics from his songs, and all were written with immense love for this little guy who touched our lives with his. Two girls – no more than thirteen or fourteen years old – were writing a lyric on the floor, and I stopped to watch them for a moment. The words were from 'Joy in Repetition', a song from Prince's 1990 album, *Graffiti Bridge*. I was impressed by their knowledge. The song was at least a decade older than them.

As we got to the Riley Creek underpass, we saw that it was covered in graffiti dedicated to Prince. Messages of condolence – many extremely personal – were everywhere. There were thousands of messages scrawled on the sloping walls and we spent a while reading this astonishing outpouring of love before we added our own. As we stood in the tunnel underneath the roaring highway above our heads, the sense of loss was palpable. All around us people were grieving. It was a surreal moment – being surrounded by people who felt exactly like I did – and once again, it reassured me to know that I was not alone in feeling like this. We headed back along the fence outside Paisley Park, and passed a guy singing a Prince tune – 'The Beautiful Ones' – at the top of his voice. He was doing the bit right at the end, which is impossible to replicate. He was giving it his best shot though. Given our surroundings, it felt like a completely natural thing to do.

We headed inside the compound at Paisley Park for day two of *Celebration 2017*, and before going in the entrance to the building, we walked the length of the Prince 4 Ever Tribute Fence again taking photos. After being given permission, I stood on the grass in front of the matching oval building that stood alongside the main edifice and Jonathan took a great picture of me. We wondered aloud about what the separate building was used for and the Paisley Park staffer told us that it was empty and had never been used for anything other than storage. He said that it may have once been pencilled in to become a basketball court, and then a prayer centre, but neither of these plans materialised. The staffer told us that the separate building wasn't made from the same material as the aluminium-panelled building we were about to go in. I looked closely, and saw that he was right. It was made of plaster.

At 4.30pm we walked through the doors of Paisley Park for the second time. It felt no less incredible than the first and again my eyes were everywhere, trying to take it all in. I headed through the corridor more quickly than last time, and as we approached the Piano Room I realised that I knew the guy in the black suit standing in front of me.

His moustache was trimmed into the same style as it was thirty-odd years ago, but he wore it with a goatee now. His hair was less wild than it used to be too, but he still looked great. His smart – not to mention expensive – black suit and tie contrasted sharply with the multitude of colours that adorned the crowd around him, and he exuded class. His name was Robert B Rivkin. To everyone here, he was known simply as Bobby Z.

Born in Minneapolis two years before his future bandleader, Bobby Z is the drummer from Prince's band, The Revolution. He played multiple instruments as a child before settling on drumming. Meeting Prince in the late '70s, he worked as a runner for the fledgling musical genius and eventually Bobby became an integral part of Prince's touring band. Prince, who had envisaged forming a multicultural group of musicians with which to surround himself, thought Bobby fitted the bill perfectly. The drummer became so important to Prince early in his career that in the liner notes of his 1978 debut LP, *For You*, Bobby is referred to as a 'Heaven-sent helper'. As Prince's sound developed, Bobby was used more frequently on his recordings, featuring on every album from 1981's *Controversy* to *Sign o' the Times* in 1987.

As we approached him, I said, "Hi Bobby", and he acknowledged me. We'd obviously never met before, but he was walking amongst the public so it felt appropriate to talk to him. I asked him if he was okay and he said, "Not really."

"I know," I replied.

He looked tense and I could see that his emotions were running high.

"This is so weird," he said to Mark, "I never thought he'd go before I did."

It was an incredibly poignant moment and I felt like I was going to cry. Bobby suffered a near fatal heart attack in 2010, and he now runs a charity called *My Purple Heart* which raises awareness of heart disease. Until Prince's passing and the reformation of The Revolution, he had played with his former bandmates only intermittently. To our surprise, Bobby walked with us through the Piano Room and into the Soundstage. I couldn't quite believe that I was talking to the drummer from The Revolution and he was talking to us like we were acquaintances. We reached the middle of the auditorium. Standing on the back row, we shook Bobby's hand, leaving him to go about his important business. I was absolutely ecstatic that we had met him. In my eyes, he is a musical legend and a fundamental part of Prince's story. Mark just looked at me in disbelief and said, "Stuart, I can't believe that just happened."

"I can," I replied. "This place is amazing."

Mark nodded in agreement.

Taking our seats, the room eventually quietened and Joel Weinshanker walked on stage. He was met with applause and thanked us, saying that we had another incredible day ahead. Then – to my astonishment – Joel quietly introduced Prince's family onto the platform. It was an extraordinary moment. Prince's actual flesh and blood were about to stand before us. They walked on stage tentatively, clearly not used to being in front of an audience of hundreds. Joel asked us to observe a minute of silence alongside Prince's siblings. As the minute mark passed, suddenly everyone was up on their feet. As Prince's family joined hands with each other, they were met with a standing ovation. They appeared genuinely touched by the gesture, and everyone in the room felt thankful to be there. Alfred Jackson – Prince's half-brother – looked out at the audience and was visibly moved. Next to him was Joel, his hands raised aloft. To his left was Norrine Nelson, Prince's half sister. Her sibling Sharon – another half-sister to Prince – stood close by. Born in 1940, she is the oldest member of Prince's surviving family. Finally, Prince's youngest sister Tyka – who bears a striking resemblance to her older brother – held hands with our host Damaris Lewis, and her infectious smile was visible from the back of the Soundstage. The family seemed overwhelmed by the reaction they were getting from us, and it was a measure of how down-to-earth they really were. I felt blessed to be in the same room as them. They left the stage, waving to us as they went.

Damaris addressed the audience, repeating her mantra from yesterday and re-emphasising our importance in passing Prince's legacy on to future generations. She said we were about to watch footage from another Prince performance that had never been seen before. This one was loaded with poignancy as it was recorded in the very room in which we were seated.

Recorded at Paisley Park on January 21st 2016, the film we watched is part of Prince's final series of shows, named the *Piano & A Microphone Tour*. This was the last performance Prince ever played at his home. As the intimate concert began, Prince was in reflective mood and he talked about his childhood and growing up with his demanding father, and also about learning to play music. He talked like I had never heard him talk before. Sometimes playful, and sometimes with his voice tinged with sadness, it was an incredibly candid performance, and as we watched this show – recorded mere months before his passing – many tears were shed.

Throughout the forty-five minute film, Prince played songs stretching right back to his early career and the new arrangements he used were supremely inventive. Watching this performance, we could see that he was truly a musical genius, and I only wished that I had been fortunate enough to have attended one of these shows. Sadly, the *Piano & A Microphone Tour* never made it as far as the UK. Prince passed away just seven days after performing in Atlanta.

As quickly as it began, the concert film ended – abruptly fading to black – and a collective sigh echoed around the arena just as it did the day before at the same moment. The Soundstage suddenly became a sea of purple people, moving to their next destination.

According to our itinerary we were due to go to the marquee for our meal, but two words appeared on the screen before us, and it made me forget about eating completely. Those words were 'The Revolution'. Forty-five minutes from now, we were due back in the Soundstage to watch Wendy Melvoin, Lisa Coleman, Brown Mark, Bobby Z, and Matt Fink talk about working with Prince. They are without question my favourite band. In fact, they have been my favourite band since I was thirteen years old.

Suddenly realising that The Revolution were doing a double header, and would be talking for ninety minutes – starting in just a few moments with a short break at the halfway point for the audience to switch with the next group – our group – I quietly told Jonathan and Ben that we were skipping the food. Mark was on the same page as me already and was going nowhere. Moving to seats near the front of the Soundstage, I offered a silent apology to the organisers of *Celebration 2017* for messing with their schedule, and we deviously turned our identification passes over so no official would spot that we were not supposed to be there. The room filled with people arriving for this event and the host – again from local radio station The Current – addressed us before welcoming the members of Prince's seminal backing band – and stars of *Purple Rain* – on to the stage. I was extremely excited at the prospect of an hour and a half listening to The Revolution talk about their relationship with Prince.

Everyone was on their feet as The Revolution took to their seats. They smiled as they received this rapturous welcome, and they looked truly humbled by the occasion. Sitting down, the host introduced them one by one. I laughed as he did so as nobody in the room really needed him to do this. The band all looked younger than their years, and I couldn't help smiling as I looked at them. These people were responsible for making my favourite music of all time. This was a huge moment for me.

As a young boy I'd watched *Purple Rain* and Prince's music promo videos relentlessly and I felt as if I knew these people as well as I knew my own friends. Growing up in a northern English town that isn't particularly known for its exotic tastes – I didn't actually know a single other *fan* – Prince was a solitary obsession for me for years. In situations I found myself in with other kids – such as discos or parties – the question would often come up, "What music do you like?", and more often than not I'd be ridiculed for liking Prince. I'd even been beaten up for it on a few occasions. I had – and still have – no idea why this happened. Prince and his band were by *far* the coolest people in my world and I was besotted. I didn't care one iota that no one else I knew got it. I'd spent a large part of my youth with the people now sitting in front of me, and those hours in my room spent writing their names and song titles in those strange fonts from the *Purple Rain* and *Around The World In A Day* album sleeves are as clear to me now – as I approach my fifties – as they were when I was a boy.

I vividly remember writing the lyrics to 'Tambourine' from *Around the World in a Day* while lying on my bed one day in 1985 – most likely within days of the album's release – and my brother suddenly coming into the room unexpectedly. I hid the piece of paper under my bed. A few hours later he found it and made fun of me mercilessly for days. He probably doesn't even remember it. But it didn't matter. As I got older, my infatuation with the band grew stronger. As a teenage boy, my attention was particularly focused on Wendy. It would be fair to say that I spent a sizeable portion of my teenage years being hopelessly in love with her. I think the racy outfits in *Purple Rain* may have played a part. Seeing her now thirty years later – along with the rest of The Revolution – all the emotions I'd felt back then came flooding back, and once again I was that fourteen year old boy, lying on my bed carefully writing their names.

The Revolution talked about how they met Prince and began working with him, and for the next ninety minutes I was in thrall. They were, by turn, friendly, argumentative, protective, affectionate, contradictory, and clearly very close, both to each other and to their fallen bandleader and mentor.

Matt Fink – dressed in his 'Dr. Fink' stage outfit of surgical scrubs, mask and stethoscope – laughed as he remembered Prince's legendary sense of humour. Prince's keyboardist since 1979, Matt was – and is – the longest serving member of The Revolution. He recounted with glee the tale of how Prince had once talked him into stealing a bullhorn from an airplane in Mississippi. Neither Prince nor Matt had realised that this was apparently a federal offence. The stolen bullhorn was discovered in Matt's bag, and he was promptly hauled from the plane. Worried about his friend, Prince admitted to officials that it had been him that had incited the theft, and he too was arrested. The pair found themselves spending the night in a local prison cell, and subsequently banned from that particular airline.

Mark Brown – aka Brown Mark – talked of how he had worked in a restaurant and had once made Prince pancakes before auditioning for the position of bassist with the band in 1981. Mark – a Minneapolitan by birth – regaled the audience with his memories of his first shows with Prince and in particular, supporting The Rolling Stones in Los Angeles in late '81. These early shows are well-known amongst Prince *fam* for all the wrong reasons. The band was subjected to horrific racial slurs and homophobic jibes. Simultaneously, they were pelted with garbage – bottles and cans being the main choice of projectile – from the hostile audience who were outraged by Prince's overtly sexual appearance – he sported bikini briefs and thigh-high legwarmers at this time – and terrified for their safety, the band fled the stage. Convinced to return for the next show, the reception they received was even worse. Word had got around, and this time the audience turned up armed with a barrage of different weapons to throw at the stage including – allegedly – a stinking bag of rotting chicken pieces. As he spoke about Prince, Mark kept his sunglasses on. I felt sure it was to hide the pain he was feeling as he talked about losing Prince, and his voice cracked as he remembered his late friend. Seconds later, his sadness turned to joy as he recalled the huge food fights that The Revolution and The Time got into with each other on tour.

Bobby Z talked about the early days, and how Prince was the most determined person he had ever met. With emotion in his voice, he recalled how Prince had urged everyone around him to do their best while doggedly rehearsing the band to near exhaustion. Bobby also spoke about how he had had to develop his drumming style when Prince introduced the Linn LM1 drum machine into the band's sound. Speaking warmly about his bandmate, Bobby said that he missed Prince every day and was thankful that he had been given the chance to work with such a singular talent.

Lisa Coleman, the pianist and keyboard player with The Revolution, told how she had joined the band in 1980, replacing the first female keyboardist, Gayle Chapman. I learned that early in her career she had been in a band with Wendy's brother, Jonathan Melvoin, who sadly passed away in 1996 when he was part of the touring line-up of the Smashing Pumpkins. Jonathan had made contributions to some of Prince's albums in the mid-'80s and was a member of Prince protégés The Family. Another member of this band was his sister – and Wendy's twin – Susannah. As we listened to her talk about her work with Prince, it struck me that Lisa was perhaps the quietest member of the band. Her tone was solemn and respectful, and she spoke eloquently. The only classically-trained member of the band, she exuded class and – like the others sat before us – she expressed gratitude for being given the opportunity to play with Prince.

Finally, Wendy Melvoin spoke. The youngest member of the band, Wendy had joined The Revolution aged just nineteen. A friend of Lisa Coleman's, Wendy was invited to audition by Prince. She brought attitude to the band, as well as being a solid guitar player. She and Lisa have known each other since childhood, and they were actually a couple during their time in The Revolution; something I was unaware of at the time. She talked at length about Prince and how she and Lisa had helped to shape his sound, opening his mind to other influences for the first time which he would incorporate into his music. Easily the most gregarious member of The Revolution, she enthused about her time with the band but at the same time was not afraid to criticise Prince for decisions she felt at the time to be wrong. She was fascinating to listen to – often talking over the other members of the band and dominating the conversation – and at one point she said something that had many in the audience, including me, close to tears. The interviewer talked about Prince's decision to dissolve The Revolution in 1986, and asked Wendy her feelings about it. She professed a profound sadness that the band ended earlier than she would have liked. Wendy thought for a moment before speaking.

"The thing about Prince," she said, "is that he was an incredible force of nature. He was like this unstoppable comet flying through the universe. And for those four or five years that we were together, we felt like we were holding on tight – just clinging on for dear life – and finally, *inevitably*, we just couldn't keep hold any longer. We felt incredibly privileged that – for a short time – he allowed his magnificent light to shine on us."

As this fascinating talk came to an end, it felt – to me at least – like they hadn't been on the stage anywhere near long enough. The interviewer left the platform and The Revolution stepped forward. The audience seized this opportunity to meet them, and we quickly headed over. The front of the stage was a writhing mass of people clamouring for a moment with their idols. Although they only stayed for a few minutes, somehow I managed a few seconds with each of them – thanking them for the impact they have had on my life – and they politely signed the back of my photo identification pass. Briefly, I held Wendy's hand, fulfilling – in part anyway – a boyhood ambition. She smiled at me and said something, but looking back now I can't even recall what it was. Just being in her orbit was enough for me. Conspicuously, Mark Brown did not stay on the stage. He preferred to leave the rest of the band behind, thus rendering my instant Revolution autograph collection incomplete forever. I didn't care though. I'd just met the greatest band of all time.

Our next event took place in the Soundstage too, so we resumed our seats and waited for it to begin. Presently, a Paisley Park staffer carried two of Prince's instruments onto the stage and placed them down carefully in the centre. A hush descended, and the next guests at *Celebration 2017* took their places. The screen displayed the words 'Prince Guitars'. I suddenly noticed that my glasses were missing from my shirt pocket. Clearly they had been lost in the crowd as we jostled for our moment with The Revolution. I figured that someone would hand them in as they were not much use to anyone unless they had exactly the same prescription as mine from their optometrist.

Two panellists were introduced by the female interviewer. Takumi Suetsugu was employed as Prince's guitar technician from the late '90s to the mid-'00s. Dave Rusan was the man responsible for creating Prince's most iconic guitar; one that has become known simply as the 'Cloud'. It is the same guitar that the American guy had bought three of at the merchandise stall the day before.

As they talked to us, the screen behind them showed images of the many guitars that Prince used throughout his career, and they pointed out interesting features about each of the instruments.

Many of them were outlandish in their appearance and had incredible paint jobs, and Takumi told us when and where they were used. Among the most extraordinary looking was the famous 'Model C' guitar. It looks like no other guitar on earth. Before long, the guitar we were all waiting to hear about inevitably came around, and Dave explained that he built the original white Cloud for Prince in 1983. The guitar is still stunning almost thirty-five years later. It's the one Apollonia buys 'The Kid' in *Purple Rain*. As I looked at the screen, I toyed with the idea of buying one from the merchandise stall. If I was ever going to own a replica Prince guitar, the Cloud would be the one. I was torn though, for I knew that if I did purchase one, my wife would not be impressed. My Prince collection already threatens to take over the house. Dave explained how – working as a luthier in the Knut-Koupee music store in Uptown Minneapolis in the early '80s – he was approached by Prince to create the guitar that would become synonymous with him. Dave explained – much to my surprise – that he only built four Cloud guitars for Prince in total. His bright yellow one sold in 2016 for over a hundred thousand dollars. He also revealed that he once auditioned – unsuccessfully – for Prince's band. He laughed at the recollection and we laughed with him.

Takumi talked about Prince's most-used guitar. It was the HS Anderson Mad Cat with the leopard-print pick guard that I saw the first time I walked into Paisley Park, and we watched a film clip that has been viewed over forty million times online. It was Prince's guitar solo during 'While My Guitar Gently Weeps', taken from the incredible Rock And Roll Hall of Fame performance in 2004. In it, he plays the Mad Cat. Despite the fact that everyone in the audience had seen this clip many times, it still caused a cheer from us all as he ended an incendiary display of guitar virtuosity. In a final act of utter nonchalance, Prince takes off the Mad Cat and throws the guitar up into the air before casually sauntering off the stage, the camera never showing who – if anyone – caught it.

To my delight, Takumi then told us who caught it. Ask me

sometime and I'll tell you what he said. As the discussion drew to a close, we remained in the Soundstage for the final event of this amazing second night at *Celebration 2017*. As the guitars were stored away, to my immense relief I spied my missing glasses. Someone had picked them up and placed them on the stage. I quickly retrieved them and headed back to my spot.

Jonathan said, "That was lucky."

He was right. I needed them to drive.

Anticipation hung heavy in the air for one of – if not *the* – biggest events of this trip and for me, one of the reasons we had got the tickets. In a few minutes, Prince's most famous backing band – The Revolution – would make history by performing live at Paisley Park. This promised to be a moment that would live with me forever. The excitement around us was palpable and as the stage technicians set up the equipment for the band, we got as close as the security around the perimeter of the stage allowed us. Finally, the moment I had waited over thirty years for was upon me. The Revolution walked onto the stage in *his* house. A new chapter in the Prince legacy was about to be written, and the crowd – like the song instructs us – went crazy.

As the band stood before us at Paisley Park, the reception The Revolution received was euphoric. As the ovation – which lasted a few minutes – subsided, in a scene eerily reminiscent of the moment Prince introduced the movie's title song at the end of *Purple Rain*, there was a brief, almost awkward silence. Wendy stepped up to the microphone and spoke. She quietly told us that the band felt that they needed to do this to help with their grief.

"We are hurting," she said. "Just like you are hurting."

She talked softly, telling the expectant audience that Prince belonged to all of us, and that we were all – as *fam* – a part of him now. She talked about the process of reforming the band, and how they had decided that they were going to take it out on the road. "Just to see what happens, and where it takes us." She stated that they were aware that no one in the band was capable of reproducing Prince's parts to his incredible standard, so they were not even going to try. She spoke deliberately, and was unapologetic in her honesty. She ended by telling us that they would give the songs that have helped define a decade their best shot, hoping that the crowd would carry them when they couldn't replicate their fallen bandleader.

With that, The Revolution launched into the spoken intro to 'Computer Blue' from *Purple Rain*.

The band hit the ground running and – given that they had performed together only sparingly over the past twelve months since Prince's passing – they were a phenomenal live outfit. Selecting cuts from their output with Prince, they played like their lives depended on it and it was amazing to see that they had lost none of their power on stage. 'Computer Blue' ended and the crowd was delirious as 'America' started up. A sea of voices rang out across the auditorium along with the band, and next to me a woman from somewhere in Scandinavia absolutely lost her mind. Next up was 'Mountains' from the 1986 *Parade* album. It has always been a favourite of mine, and seeing the band perform it up close was just incredible. It was made even more special by the addition of Wendy's twin sister, Susannah Melvoin, who suddenly appeared onstage. Looking sensational in a wide-brimmed fedora and skin-tight black jeans, she danced and sang like a woman possessed. Somehow, she also seemed untouched by the passage of time and still looked like she was in '86. She stayed for the remainder of the show. Then from out of nowhere, the band dropped a super deep cut that was strictly for the hardcore *fam*. 'Our Destiny' and 'Roadhouse Garden' – both originally recorded in 1984 – are a pair of songs that remained officially unreleased until 2017. In fact, they remained unreleased for a further two months after the performance I was watching right then. Both songs finally got their moment to shine in June 2017 as part of the amazing *Purple Rain* reissue – remastered by Prince himself – that was released to critical acclaim. As the songs – they were performed as a medley – began, a roar of delight went up from the Prince aficionados in the crowd and everyone danced, totally lost in the moment. Wendy needn't have worried about The Revolution's performance. It was *sensational*.

Running through 'Raspberry Beret' and the killer B-side that should have been a hit, 'Erotic City', the band threw a curveball at us in the shape of Prince's 1981 single 'Let's Work' from his *Controversy* album. It surprised me when it started. I was not expecting them to play anything this early from Prince's canon. It's a stunning song – one of his very best in my opinion – and it has a sound that is quintessentially *Prince*. The band tore through 'Let's Work' with aplomb, joined onstage by Stokley Williams from the band Mint Condition. Stokley's voice is perfect for the task, and he strutted around the stage like Prince in his prime. Like Susannah, Stokley stayed onstage for the rest of the gig. '1999' followed, with 'Paisley Park' hot on its heels. At one point during it, Wendy fluffed a line, and looked at the rest of the band laughing. They grinned back at her. Nobody cared. After another early cut, 'Controversy', the band suddenly stopped dead, and the audience did too.

Wendy changed her electric guitar for an acoustic, and approaching the microphone she cleared her voice and told us the story of the recording of the heartbreaking 'Sometimes It Snows in April'. The song was written and recorded quickly – in just one day – and features input from just Prince, Wendy, and Lisa. The number received significant attention on the day of Prince's passing, as it was recorded thirty-one years to the day earlier. She asked that we be patient with her as she sang it, confessing that she didn't know if she would make it all the way through without breaking down.

The song began and an absolute stillness descended on the room. As she played, I could hear people weeping, gently. I tried to hold my emotions in check but it was no use. Tears began to fall down my face, and as Wendy performed this amazing, beautiful song, she started to cry softly too. She was one with her audience, and for a few minutes, we were on a level with her that none of us had ever experienced before. She stood alongside us not just as a Prince colleague, but as Prince *fam*. The room was caught up in a torrent of emotion and it was truly a moment that I doubt any of us will forget. I don't ever recall crying at a concert before, but this was a special night. 'Sometimes It Snows in April' is an especially poignant number too. The song's lyric tells the story of Christopher Tracy, Prince's character from the *Under the Cherry Moon* movie. The narrator explains the effect Tracy's death has had on them, and they express their wish to meet him again in the afterlife. It is a stunning song and Wendy's performance was – without exception – the most heartfelt thing I have ever witnessed on a stage.

As the song ended, she was in floods of tears. The April 21st 2017 performance of 'Sometimes It Snows in April' was not just a *Celebration 2017* high watermark, it was without doubt one of the greatest musical moments of my life.

As the crowd recovered, the band began the intro to 'Let's Go Crazy' from *Purple Rain* before launching into the song full-throttle. The famous guitar solo was intact and while it was not as accomplished as a Prince solo – what could be? – it sent the audience into a frenzy. After this – just like the end of the movie – the show climaxed with three songs. Their position in the set list's running order was never in doubt.

We stood transfixed as the opening chords of the epic 'Purple Rain' rang out and as one of Prince's most recognisable – and universal – songs unfurled toward its dramatic crescendo, the audience were hand-in-hand, embracing each other and caught in a collective moment of tenderness. The love felt for Prince at Paisley Park – and each other – on the first anniversary of his passing was undeniable.

Suddenly, the band was back in party mode and 'I Would Die 4 U' turned the entire auditorium into a discothèque. The final song of the night, 'Baby I'm a Star', was a triumphant end to proceedings, and as the band took a bow and thanked everyone for being there, the audience were on their feet. After nearly two hours on stage, The Revolution had proved to every one of us there that they were a formidable team even without their leader. They left the stage to a standing ovation, waving and smiling as they went.

The house lights came up and the audience felt like they had been on an emotional rollercoaster ride. Everyone had an equal measure of joy and sadness written on their faces. As I stood in Prince's home with Jonathan, Ben and Mark, we looked at each other. We had truly witnessed Minneapolis music history, and it was a show I'll never forget.

Heading outside into the night, we strode purposefully back to the car. Picking up our candles – I'd bought one for Mark too – we headed back to the underpass outside Paisley Park. It was dark and a procession of people were walking to the Riley Creek tunnel, in order to attend the midnight candlelit vigil. The underpass had taken on a different personality in the dark. It was an incredibly poignant place to be. As we walked into the tunnel, there were dozens of candles at our feet, placed there by *fam*. The whole underpass flickered in the soft light. Mark saw Prince's Love Symbol marked out on the floor in candles at the far end of the underpass, and we added our candles to it and took photos. As we stood in the underpass under Highway 5, a woman approached us. She introduced herself and told me that she was a reporter from a radio station in New Zealand. I'd spotted her photo identification pass earlier in the day. She'd hastily scribbled something on the back to notify officials at *Celebration 2017* that she was a broadcaster. As she spoke to me, I knew that she was a big Prince *fam*. She'd been very emotional inside. Everyone had noticed. Prince's passing had obviously affected her deeply. She asked if I would like to be interviewed for her station and opened her bag to reveal a huge tape recorder. To her surprise, I turned down her request. Taken aback, she asked why I didn't want to speak on the record. I told her that I was too emotional to converse coherently with her right now. Mark – who is far more gregarious than I am – volunteered to be recorded, and he spoke about what Prince meant to him. After they were done, we decided to leave the vigil. It was not yet midnight, but none of us had eaten since breakfast, and it was approaching 11.00pm. As we walked back to the car, I remarked that it was strange that Sheila Escovedo – Sheila E – Prince's post-Revolution drummer, had been strangely absent during *Celebration 2017*. She'd been all over the news when he had passed, and as one of his closest confidants – they'd even been engaged at one point – I'd expected her to be here. Mark immediately said that she was performing in Florida tonight. He had evidently thought the same thing and checked.

Driving the short distance back to our hotel on West 78th Street, we elected to go back to Chuck Wagon Charlie's Smokehouse and Saloon to see our old friend Shane. To our dismay, we found that it was closed for the evening. Ben recalled that there was a restaurant on the other side of the hotel that did chicken wings. Ben loves chicken wings. He also loved this particular place and was familiar with it already, albeit not in Chanhassen. He vacations regularly in Florida and often goes to the same restaurant when he's in the Sunshine State.

Walking to Buffalo Wild Wings at 550 West 79th Street, the Chanhassen avenues were silent. As we turned a corner, we were outside Walgreens, one of the local pharmacies where Prince had allegedly picked up medication a few days before his passing. I stopped outside the Chemist and looked up at the sign.

"This might be one of the last places he ever went to," I said to no one in particular.

Walking into the huge restaurant, we expected to see it empty at that time of night, but there were a few tables taken. The waitress showed us to a booth and took our order. I ordered a sharing platter of various tasters, Jonathan and Mark opted for burgers, and Ben chose a ridiculous amount of chicken wings and expertly selected appropriate sauces to accompany them. This guy knows his stuff. Our server picked up on our English accents – everyone here did – and she came back over to ask why we were in Chanhassen. Explaining that we were there for *Celebration*

2017 and showing her our photo identification passes – which we were still wearing – she told us that she was a big Prince fan when she was younger. She also talked about the aftermath of his passing, and said that the quiet suburb had been full of reporters and police.

"Very sad," she said.

As the restaurant was quiet, she spent longer talking to us than she normally would, I suspect, and she seemed genuinely interested as we told her about all of the events we had attended on our trip.

I asked her if she had ever seen Prince around town.

"Only once," she told me. She recounted her Prince-related incident, excitedly telling us that she saw him in a supermarket just behind the building we were in. "It was a few years ago now," she began. "It was two or three in the morning, and I had just finished my shift. I went in to pick up some things, and the place was totally empty. As I was leaving, Prince walked in. He had his security with him and he had a girl on each arm. They were beautiful," she said, "and very young." She laughed and headed off to clear some tables.

Presently, our food arrived and we talked about the associates of Prince we hadn't seen in Minneapolis. I talked about Maceo Parker – Prince's saxophonist throughout the '00s – who was a member of James Brown's band in his younger days. I last saw him with Prince in 2007 at the *21 Nights in London* shows at the O2 in Greenwich, a series of concerts in support of the *Planet Earth* album. Prince performed to over 350,000 *fam* in London, and his residency at the former Millennium Dome is a record that still stood at the time of writing. Mark talked about Rhonda Smith, the bassist who spent ten years in Prince's band. Rhonda worked on the sprawling thirty-six track *Emancipation* album, the first released after his contract with Warner Bros was dissolved in 1996. The album running time is three hours, to the second. Again, it had been years since I last saw Rhonda with Prince. We finished our meals, and left the restaurant. Walking back to the Country Inn and Suites, we reflected on the day and – in particular The Revolution – and I felt on top of the world to have been one of the relatively few people to be inside Prince's house on this important anniversary.

Arriving in the hotel lobby, we spotted a notice on the wall informing us that Shelby J from the NPG would be doing an album signing in the conference room of the hotel in the morning. We bid each other goodnight, and retired to our rooms where I called my wife. She had just got up. It was 7.00am back in the UK. She said that she was missing me, and as we talked we suddenly realised that today marked the longest time we had ever been apart. I told her I'd be home soon. She said goodnight and hung up, and I sent her the photos I'd taken. I grabbed a quick shower and flicked the TV on, before quickly falling asleep. Tomorrow I'd be in the same room as The Time – Prince protégés and stars of *Purple Rain* – and I couldn't wait.

SATURDAY

After the now customary huge breakfast, we headed to the conference room where Shelby J was signing copies of her new album, *10*. Although it wasn't on general sale yet, she was letting her fans – in town for the anniversary of Prince's passing – have them a little early. We joined the queue as Shelby met people and chatted to each of them for a few minutes. I grabbed a copy of her CD and waited in line. Mark – who was ahead of me in the queue – sat with Shelby just before I did. He talked about Prince and she started crying. Wiping her eyes, she gave him a hug and he moved off so I could talk to her. As I sat down, she hugged me and I told her how great the show at the Dakota was and how we'd met Monica. She thanked me and we chatted about Prince for a minute or two which resulted in more tears. She wiped her eyes and laughed, playfully telling me off for making her cry again after Mark had done the same thing. She signed my CD and I also got a bracelet from her. It's made from dark purple stones and has a little silver pendant hanging from it. On one side of it is Prince's Love Symbol. The reverse has a symbol designed by Shelby. We hugged again and Jonathan took a brilliant photo of us before I headed over to say hello to Monica who was nearby.

We were due to begin day three of *Celebration 2017* at Paisley Park at 11.00am, so we had a little time to relax in the hotel lobby before setting off. Mark was leaving us after our day at Paisley Park today. He had booked accommodation at another hotel in Downtown Minneapolis for the rest of his stay. We decided to travel to *Celebration 2017* separately and Mark went up to his room to pack his things. We agreed to meet in an hour at the spot on Park Road behind Paisley Park where we had parked the day before. Mark was going to head off to his next hotel after we finished.

I drove the short distance to Paisley Park and with impeccable timing Mark pulled up sixty seconds later. He and Jonathan were both wearing paisley-patterned shirts and they laughed as they compared them.

Walking into Prince's home for day three of *Celebration 2017*, we headed straight for the Soundstage and took our seats. Damaris Lewis welcomed us with her now familiar, "Listen. Learn. Teach. Love," mantra and – as per the previous two days – we first watched a clip of Prince performing live. The announcement that today's show was a *Purple Rain Tour* performance from Florida in 1985 drew a huge cheer from the audience. Again, it had never been seen in public before, and for a moment I let that incredible information sink in. The piece of film we were about to enjoy had been sitting in Prince's vault for thirty-two years, until now.

Damaris Lewis left the stage and the film opened with 'Delirious' from Prince's 1982 album, *1999*. The show, filmed at Miami's Orange Bowl stadium – dubbed the 'Purple Bowl' for this event – is the final concert of the *Purple Rain Tour*, recorded on April 7th 1985. The band was in triumphant end-of-tour spirits and Prince was at his playful best with the audience, whipping them to frenzy with salacious gestures and comments. As he and the band ripped through the double whammy of *1999*'s title track and the album's next song 'Little Red Corvette', his performance was astonishing, and I realised that – as we watched this masterful performer at work – it was as powerful now as it was in 1985. The gorgeous 'Do Me, Baby' – one of my favourite Prince numbers – from 1981's *Controversy* album followed 'Take Me With U' from *Purple Rain*, and then 'Irresistible Bitch', the b-side of 'Let's Pretend We're Married', *1999*'s final single. Prince's homage to James Brown was next. 'Possessed', a song that was originally recorded in 1983, is a ten minute long phenomenal funk workout that did not see an official release until the 2017 reissue of the *Purple Rain* soundtrack, which includes it on a bonus disc. In my opinion it is one of his finest unreleased numbers, and live it was just incredible. Prince pulled out his best 'Godfather of Soul' moves, whooping and growling which sent the crowd wild throughout the song. Prince then sat at his purple piano and performed a dramatic version of 'How Come U Don't Call Me Any More?', the non-album b-side of the '1999' single which was covered in 2001 by Alicia Keys. Asking the audience to sing along, Prince hit just about every high note in his repertoire before abruptly halting the song, and adopting the sassy persona of a jilted boyfriend asking the audience why they don't call him. For the next few minutes, with only minimal accompaniment from The Revolution – it was basically just keyboard – he was downright *filthy*, ultimately asking them if they have another man. "Is he fine?" he enquired, turning his back to the adoring masses. "Tell me. Does a man have an ass like mine?" The audience roared its approval. It was an exhilarating performance. Prince was a man at the peak of his powers and he absolutely knew it. Although the footage is over thirty years old, it still sent shivers down my spine. The last number we saw was 'Temptation' from the psychedelia-tinged *Around the World in a Day* album. Interestingly, the album was not actually released at this point. It hit stores on April 22nd 1985, a few weeks after this performance. In reality, Prince had already recorded his next album before the current *Purple Rain* promotional push had even ended. The audience inside the Soundstage at Paisley Park sang along with the film, and as the spectacular film ended, the familiar communal sigh went up yet again.

We were to stay in the Soundstage for our next event, which was a panel discussion with Prince's studio engineers. The giant screen showed three names. One of them was a legend amongst Prince *fam*.

We were sitting twenty feet from the stage as Pete Rhodes from the Black Music America Network introduced Susan Rogers, Chris James, and Dylan Dresdow onto the stage. Susan is perhaps the most well-known engineer to have worked with Prince. She later became an Associate Professor at Berklee College of Music in Boston. Working with Prince from 1983 to 1988, Susan was instrumental in the development of Prince's sound.

Susan told us how she first heard Prince in the late '70s – hearing 'Soft and Wet' on a bus – and immediately fell in love with his music. In 1983, while Prince was beginning to record the *Purple Rain* album, he expressed to his management team the desire to work with a more experienced studio tech. Susan had the experience he was looking for. Word of this reached Susan's boyfriend at the time, who worked in Westlake Recording Studios in Hollywood. He volunteered Susan for the role and she leapt at the opportunity to work with Prince. After being interviewed by his management team, the job was hers. Moving to Minneapolis, she began a relationship with Prince that she describes as, "A dream come true."

Speaking warmly about her friend and former employer, Susan talked about how Prince was like a finely-tuned machine in the studio, barely eating, keeping irregular hours, and always ready to record whenever the desire would take him, no matter where or when. She laughed as she told us that often she would be at home in bed in the middle of the night and the phone would ring and it would be Prince on the line who would say simply, "See you in an hour," before putting the phone down. Susan would get dressed and drive to his house to record. While working on *Purple Rain*, Susan told us how she was incredibly excited for the public to hear the new songs they had been working on. Often Prince would send the rest of the band home after a day in the studio, and he and Susan would work alone. She recounted a tale about Prince recording a guitar solo and – making a rare mistake – he had asked her to roll the tape back to record a portion of the solo again. As she watched him play, she wasn't sure when to hit the record button as he hadn't cued her to do so. She hit record – making the decision herself – and Prince immediately stopped playing. He paused the tape machine and asked her, "Who cued you in?" Susan – embarrassed by her mistake – rolled the tape back and readied herself again for the take. "Watch me," said Prince. As he played the solo they looked at each other, and she saw him lift his head slowly and then drop it at the moment he wanted her to hit record. She said that after that, they developed an almost telepathic understanding in the studio.

As Susan talked, she was incredibly self-deprecating, and she played down her importance in Prince's work. Everyone watching knew this, and, as I listened to her talk, I realised I was sitting in front of the woman who was partly responsible for the invention of Prince's famous alter-ego, 'Camille' in 1986. She told the audience that one time during a recording session, she noticed that the tape was running at the wrong speed and was worried Prince would be upset about having to re-record his vocal. Upon hearing the resulting tape – and his voice sounding like he was inhaling helium – he decided he liked the effect it had produced, and asked her to do it again. As a direct result of this originally unintentional studio error, Prince performed as 'Camille' on several songs from the 1987 *Sign o' the Times* album, most notably the superb cut 'If I Was Your Girlfriend'. In fact, Prince liked the distorted vocal effect so much that he planned an entire album based on the character of 'Camille', but the project was shelved before completion. Several tracks were ultimately selected for *Sign o' the Times*, and the remaining unused ones surfaced later in non-album track releases such as b-sides and film soundtracks.

'Wally' is a song that Prince recorded a few days after Christmas 1986. The number chronicles the breakup of a relationship between Prince and a woman – presumably Susannah Melvoin – and in it he thanks 'Wally' for being a friend. Susan told the story of how Prince – working alone in the studio – decided the song was too personal and in an effort to change the feel of it, began layering additional percussion over the top of the recording, eventually rendering it unrecognisable from its original form. Susan recalled that she felt the song was one of the strongest tracks Prince had ever cut, and was dismayed when – at the end of the session – he asked her to erase all twenty four channels. She pleaded with Prince not to lose the song, but he insisted, and she sadly erased the song from history.

Susan talked about the legendary vault at Paisley Park that reportedly contains hundreds of songs, films, and ephemera that Prince did not release during his lifetime. She told us that she began compiling Prince's work in the vault a long time ago and hoped that one day this unseen work would see the light of day. She also talked about a track that had only recently been released, shortly after Prince's passing. 'Moonbeam Levels' is a song that was originally recorded in 1982, and until its inclusion in the 2016 *Prince 4ever* compilation, it remained locked in the vault – Prince reportedly always unsure which album to release it on. Susan ended by saying that working with Prince was the pinnacle of her career, and she felt incredibly lucky to have been given the chance to spend five years in the studio with him.

Chris James is a Grammy-nominated engineer and guitarist who worked with Prince throughout the latter part of his career, most notably performing studio duties on the *Hitnrun Phase Two* album from 2016. The album was first made available publicly on CD at the two *Piano & A Microphone* shows at Paisley Park on January 21st. The very copy I own is from those shows. As well as *Hitnrun Phase Two*, Chris also mixed 2014's *Art Official Age* and *Plectrumelectrum*, the two studio albums Prince released simultaneously in September of that year. He spoke of Prince with affection and told how he was a master in the studio, able to switch from performance to sitting at the recording console in a moment, leaving the young producer in awe. Chris echoed Susan Rogers, saying that the vault contained a treasure trove of material that had yet to see the light of day, much of which was recorded right up to Prince's passing.

Dylan Dresdow, aka '3-D', is an Emmy award-winning mixer who has worked with some of the biggest names in popular music, including Michael Jackson and Madonna. Along with Chris he worked as the producer on *Hitnrun Phase Two*. He talked about his experiences of working with Prince, saying that of the list of illustrious artists he had worked with, Prince was the most naturally gifted of them all.

From the Soundstage we moved to the NPG Music Club next door for our next panel discussion. This one was focused on Prince's fashion. The panel was comprised of Kim Berry, Prince's hairstylist for twenty eight years, Stacia Lang, a costume designer who worked at Paisley Park for several years during the nineties, Debbie McGuan, Prince's long-time designer, and Arturo Padilla, who worked as Prince's tailor. During their Q&A session, the screen behind them showed various photos of Prince's outfits and pages from Debbie and Stacia's design scrapbooks. The illustrations revealed some of the incredible stage costumes and fashion designs that they came up with for Prince and his band members. Some of the outfits were recognisable as ones Prince wore during his lifetime, and others were ones that never made it past the drawing board stage.

Stacia laughed as she recounted the episode where she designed Prince's infamous costume from his performance of 'Gett Off' at the 1991 MTV Music Awards. It was the yellow suit with the cut-out butt. She originally made two designs, one revealing much more than the other. Prince picked the one offering the most coverage. If you watch the clip you can see that the one he chose doesn't leave much to the imagination, so one can only wonder what the other must have looked like.

The panel discussed working with Prince, and how he was always willing to give them free rein to come up with whatever they thought would make him look good. Showing a genuine adoration for Prince, Kim Berry – perhaps the female employee who got closer to him than any other – had an infectious charm that lit up the room. She was by turns both hilarious and incredibly touching – her eyes filled with tears as she spoke – and she laughed when she revealed how Prince would often decide to do spur of the moment things to his hair – like shaving a crude chunk out of it above his ear – and then ask Kim to finish the job to an acceptable standard. She also told how he would grow his hair for two years at a time and then promptly ask her to cut it all off. She would beg him to keep it, but said he always got his way. When Kim laughed, they could hear it in the next room. She kept the audience in thrall with her funny stories and was totally down to earth. She described how she first met Prince who – upon offering her the job – said she needed to trim her long nails.

"I cut them off right there and then in front of him," she joked, "and he burst out laughing."

Kim also told us the story of how, one day, Prince was having his hair done and Kim's young daughter was in the room. She was wearing a pair of those fashionable sneakers that have flashing lights in the heels. Prince loved them, and he took one of the shoes from Kim's daughter and began studying it. Kim recalled that he wondered aloud about the possibility of a pair being made in an adult size for him. Of course, being Prince, they could, and the resulting shoes – which Prince wore many times – sat alongside Kim on the stage.

As well as designing his costumes, Debbie McGuan was also the woman responsible for designing the artwork for some of Prince's albums in the mid-'90s. The drawings on the cover of the NPG's *Exodus* album from 1995 are examples of Debbie's work, and she continued to design the packaging of his music releases through to '98's *New Power Soul* album. The sleeve for the cover of *20Ten* – the album Prince gave away free with a British newspaper that year – also features her artwork.

Arturo Padilla is a Mexican tailor who designed many beautiful custom outfits for Prince. Some of the outfits he created were on the stage next to him as he spoke. Arturo told us anecdotes about his time working for Prince and remembered him with obvious affection. He laughed as he remembered when Prince would sometimes ask for clothing that was particularly outlandish, and said he quickly learned not to be surprised at anything he was required to create. When the discussion ended, the panel talked to several members of the audience as the room cleared.

It was 1.45pm. According to our itinerary, we were now supposed to head to the marquee for food, but again we went off-course, and followed our own plan. Sorry again, Joel. Ben elected to stay in the marquee – as did Mark – while Jonathan and I headed outside to the parking lot in front of Paisley Park to take photos of the Prince 4 Ever Tribute Fence and the complex while there was no one else around to get in the shot. As we went outside, a member of staff asked us if we would like our phones unlocking from their pouches and we quickly headed to the facade of the building.

As suspected, the grounds of Paisley Park were now empty. We walked over to the fence and began taking photos. We also took some wonderful shots of the building itself, and us stood outside it. I looked through the entrance doors and I could see that another party of *Celebration 2017* attendees were having a tour of the building. We were due to go on our tour tomorrow.

Heading back to the marquee, we had ten minutes until our final event of our third day at *Celebration 2017*, so we decided to go back into the Soundstage to watch the last few minutes of a panel discussion that was taking place there.

Sal Greco and Mark 'Red' White are former members of Paisley Park staff who worked at the recording complex from the *Sign o' the Times* era to the mid-'90s. Sal – who was employed as a technical engineer – talked about his time as an associate of Prince's. He served as engineer on Sheila E's second solo album, *In Romance 1600*, even further back, in 1985 before the complex existed in Chanhassen. Mark – or 'Red' as he is simply known – talked about the building of Paisley Park and the input that Prince had in its design.

We didn't catch much of this panel sadly before the lights went up and the stage cleared, ready for the main event of the day. We were about to witness one of the greatest – not to mention funniest – funk bands of all time live in concert. This was a first for me and a first for them too as they had never played at Paisley Park before. The anticipation in the audience was incredible as we awaited the arrival of Mr Morris E Day and Minneapolis legends The Time on stage.

In 1981, Prince's record label – Warner Brothers – was pleased with the way his career was progressing. To show their appreciation, they inserted a clause in his contract that allowed him to recruit other artists and nurture them as part of their artist roster. This allowed the young musician – who was now on the threshold of stardom – another avenue to release his material, giving him the freedom to explore other genres of music within his own records.

The first group Prince recruited was a Minneapolis band named Flyte Tyme. A staple of the Minneapolis club circuit, they were a funk outfit that included Jimmy 'Jam' Harris and Terry Lewis. The pair would go on to phenomenal success later in the '80s as one of the most in-demand production teams in popular music, working with a plethora of superstars, most notably Janet Jackson. In 1981 however, they were unknown outside of Minnesota's music scene. An earlier line-up of the band had also included singer Cynthia Johnson. In 1980, before Prince's involvement with Flyte Tyme, Cynthia had left the band and joined another Minneapolis group, Lipps Inc, who reached the number one spot on single charts around the world with 'Funkytown'. Her replacement in Flyte Tyme was one Alexander O'Neal. Prince – seizing his opportunity to produce an outfit that could front his R&B and funk numbers – created a brand new band, adding guitarist Jesse Johnson to the line-up, and replacing Alexander with Morris Day, the drummer from Prince's early band Grand Central. Thus, The Time was born. Alexander O'Neal went on to enjoy a successful career of his own, having many hits including the brilliant 'Fake' and 'Criticize' singles from his 1987 album *Hearsay*. The album was produced by Jimmy 'Jam' Harris, his former Flyte Tyme bandmate. On a related note, I sang 'Criticize' on stage with Alexander O'Neal – an spent an hour chatting with him backstage – at a show in the UK in 2016. We didn't discuss Prince.

The Time went on to become arguably the most successful

of Prince's associated acts, achieving several chart hits including 'Jungle Love' – a track they perform on celluloid in *Purple Rain* – and 'Jerk Out', the track taken back from Mazarati, which hit the Billboard Hot 100 Top Ten in 1990. Interestingly, Prince's original recording of 'Jerk Out' – which features him performing all vocals and instruments – remains unreleased at the time of writing.

Morris Day – singer with the Time – is one of the truly great characters of the Prince story. Originally the drummer in funk outfit Grand Central alongside Prince and André Anderson, Morris quickly developed a playboy persona on stage. He began dressing like a 1940's gangster, adopting sharp pinstripe suits with exaggerated inverted triangle silhouettes and black-and-white wingtip shoes into his stage costumes. Coupled with his perfectly coiffed hair and neatly trimmed moustache, Morris looked every inch a star.

In *Purple Rain*, Morris plays the comic foil to Prince's sensitive character, and subsequently enjoys some of the best lines in the film, many of which are centred on his relationship with his faithful manservant, Jerome Benton. The duo threatens to steal the entire movie, and critics at the time particularly praised Morris' performance, citing his natural flair for comedy as one of the movie's greatest qualities. Morris and Jerome – brother of Flyte Tyme's Terry Lewis – continued this double act on stage when The Time performed, and Morris' exaggerated vanity and comedic bravado – particularly with women – endeared him hugely to audiences. The sight of his valet carrying a large mirror on stage mid-number – in order for Morris to check his hair – was a moment of absolute brilliance which drew huge cheers from the audience. Coincidentally, like Morris in *Purple Rain*, Jerome Benton was also given his time to shine on the silver screen.

In 1986, Prince gave him a co-starring role in his second movie, the sumptuous romantic comedy *Under the Cherry Moon*. Sadly, the film – shot in the South of France and released in black-and-white – failed to build on Prince's bankability at the box office and largely signalled the end of his career as a serious actor. Speaking as a Prince *fam*, *Under the Cherry Moon* may not have pleased film critics, but it remains a great little movie that is exquisitely shot. Whenever I watch it, I thoroughly enjoy it, as does every other *fam* I know.

On Saturday April 22nd 2017, The Time walked onto the stage to perform at Paisley Park for the first time in their history. The crowd was on its feet cheering wildly as the band took their positions at their instruments. Waving to the audience, Morris Day still looked incredible. Sixty years old this year, he was the epitome of cool. As sharply dressed as he was in his *Purple Rain* days, his white pinstripe suit with huge shoulder pads and arctic-white knee length overcoat made him look like a cross between a '70's pimp and a gangster rapper. His hair was a bit shorter than it was in '84, and his face had aged a touch – he didn't take off his sunglasses until midway through the show – but he was still unmistakeably *Morris*.

Before the performance began, Morris gave thanks to the man who gave him his big break. It was an incredibly heartfelt moment and he pointed to the Love Symbol at the back of the room as he talked to Prince. He was visibly moved. Then – in a surprising opening number choice that delighted us – the band launched into a cover version of Prince's '82 hit, '1999'. Their playing was unbelievably tight, and it was clear that The Time was as good a funk outfit now as they had ever been. Sadly, it appeared that Jerome's role as valet to Morris had been taken by someone else – for this performance his shoes were filled by Sylvester Donald – but the synchronised dance moves and comedy flourishes remained intact and were performed with astonishing accuracy. We laughed as Morris joked to Sylvester that he better not stand on his shoes.

Between numbers, Morris performed little skits, his braggadocio and interaction with the crowd causing huge laughter and applause. During one such moment, he compared himself – somewhat bizarrely – to a bottle of bubbly. Dripping with perspiration from his energetic moves and multi-layered stage outfit, he wiped his forehead with a silk handkerchief from his breast pocket and asked the audience if they thought he was sweating. The audience responded in the affirmative. Morris shook his head. He then asked if we had ever noticed that a cold bottle of champagne – when taken out of the refrigerator – develops a film of tiny water droplets on the glass surface of the bottle.

"That's called *condensating*, baby," said Morris – oblivious to the fact that there's no such word – "And that's what I'm doing. No, no, no, this ain't sweat, honey. Morris is just *condensating*."

It was a genuinely hilarious moment, and I spotted that even Morris thought it was funny as a wry smile appeared on his face, breaking his cool character just for a second.

The band covered numbers from their entire back catalogue and the crowd roared when classics like 'Get It Up', and 'Cool' from their debut self-titled 1981 LP appeared in the set. At one point Morris introduced the band, and an enormous cheer went up for original members Jellybean Johnson on drums and Monty Moir on keys. Running through almost every track on their 1982 album, *What Time Is It?*, the band was incredible. Everyone in the room was dancing wildly, including me. I couldn't believe that I was finally seeing The Time perform live. It had taken three quarters of my life to arrive at this moment. I turned to Mark who was grinning at me manically and clearly having the time of his life. He obviously couldn't believe it either.

At one point in the show, Morris got a woman up out of the audience and asked her to pretend she lusted after The Time's guitarist, Torell 'Tori' Ruffin. Morris asked her to "Give Tori the come-on, baby," but warned her not to, "Give all your goodies up straight away."

The woman smiled and – showing no inhibitions whatsoever – started dancing provocatively in front of Tori, who approached her. She immediately threw herself into his arms, and Morris interjected at once. "No baby, you gotta make him beg for you. Don't make it easy for him and give in straight away."

Again she danced, and as before she threw herself at the

bemused Tori, who looked at the crowd while shrugging his shoulders and grinning.

Morris took her hand once more. "Look, baby. You want him, and he wants you. Just be cool, and don't let him know that you want him. Make him work for it," he said.

The woman started dancing again and as Tori approached her for the third time she threw herself at him yet again. Morris looked at the audience – totally deadpan – and simply pursed his lips, exactly like he does in *Purple Rain*. It was one of many brilliant comedy moments throughout the performance which left the audience in hysterics. The woman started laughing along with us, and Morris abandoned the skit completely – laughing himself by now – before signalling to the band who launched into the remainder of the song. She remained onstage for the rest of the number, dancing with The Time.

A short while later, Morris invited a conga line of around thirty audience members onto the stage and they danced for all they were worth. It was a glorious moment for them, to be on stage with this incredible band, which was so instrumental in Prince's life and work. Amongst the audience members on the stage, I spotted the American guy who had bought the Cloud guitars on day one of *Celebration 2017*.

It was inevitable that the Time's show ended with arguably their two biggest numbers, 'The Bird', and 'Jungle Love'. Both tracks are taken from their best-selling 1984 album, *Ice Cream Castle*, and they are also performed by the band in the *Purple Rain* movie. As Morris did the familiar dance move to 'The Bird', flapping his arms, the audience copied him and we sang along to the chorus. It was like the scene from *Purple Rain* all over again. The biggest cheer of the night went up when 'Jungle Love' began. Morris did his best kookaburra impression and the audience lost its collective mind. The song was still an absolute monster jam, and Morris and Sylvester did the famous dance step from the movie – kicking their legs out in unison – mirroring each other exactly. It was an utterly brilliant dance-floor move. Jerome Benton did the same one many times with Prince on the

Purple Rain Tour. I tried to replicate it years ago when I was a good deal younger. It's incredibly hard to do. We revelled in the glorious thumping bass-line and stabbing synthesizers and sang at the top of our voices. The chant in the chorus rang out around the Soundstage at Paisley Park, before Tori let rip with a brilliant guitar solo which brought the house down. After an exhilarating ninety minutes, the breathtaking show was over. His luxurious overcoat draped over his shoulders like some modern day James Brown, Morris Day waved to us as he left the stage. The show was an absolute triumph.

As the lights came up, I turned to Mark.

He looked at me and said, "Stu, we've just seen The Time," and he grinned from ear to ear.

It was a glorious end to our third day at *Celebration 2017*.

It was still only 4.00pm, so our day was far from over. Leaving Paisley Park, we walked along Audubon Road and headed back to the cars. Mark had packed his bag and it was in his car so he could head straight to his next hotel which was located Downtown. We hugged and agreed to meet at the same spot tomorrow at 4.00pm for our final day at *Celebration 2017*. He set off with a wave. I said we should head back to our hotel on West 78th Street in Chanhassen as the book signing by Alex Hahn and Laura Tiebert was currently taking place.

During the drive back to the hotel, we chattered excitedly about how amazing the day had been. We all agreed that this trip was the greatest thing we'd ever done. Jonathan joked that vacations were ruined for life for him after this, as no other trip could ever live up to the week we'd had so far. Ben agreed. At this point – and now that Mark had left us – I apologised to them both as I felt like I'd neglected them a little while Mark had been around. I explained that I felt it was important to get as much as I could out of my time with him, as I wasn't sure when – if ever – I would see him again after this trip. Luckily, my companions understood and graciously said I had nothing to apologise for. Like I said at the beginning of this book, they're both great guys.

We arrived back at the hotel, and I popped up to my room to get the books Alex and Laura had written. Putting them in my bag, I met Jonathan and Ben downstairs, and we headed to the same conference room where we had previously met Shelby J.

The conference room had long tables running down the sides and on them were plates of cookies. The cookies were purple, pink, and yellow, and had Prince's song titles iced onto them. I spotted Alex chatting and headed over to Laura who was on the other side of the room. We talked for five minutes, and she asked where I had travelled from. She asked about my accent, saying it wasn't like any other English accent she'd heard. I told her I was from the north.

"I sound Scottish, don't I?" I asked.

"You do!" she replied, smiling.

We talked about Prince and she told me how she had been a *fam* growing up. I asked Laura where she lived and she said that she had moved to Chanhassen from Illinois with her husband and children.

"Wow," I said. "You must be a huge fan."

She laughed and said that she was.

After a few minutes talking, I asked her to sign my book, and Jonathan grabbed a photo of us together. I thanked Laura and she took me over to Alex Hahn. Laura introduced me and we spoke about their new book for a few minutes. He signed my copy underneath Laura's signature and I surprised him by pulling my other book – his first Prince biography, *Possessed – The Rise and Fall of Prince* – out of my bag. He was taken aback when he saw it and asked where I had got it from. I told Alex that I had brought it from England at the last minute, and I had owned it since its publication fourteen years ago in 2003.

"Really?" he said. "It looks like new!"

I laughed and told him that my Prince books had their own bookcase, which made him chuckle. "Can you sign it for me?" I asked.

He looked at me. "Are you sure?" he said. "It's a really rare book now and worth a few hundred dollars."

I said that I was sure and he signed it, '*To Stuart, Thank U, Alex.*'

I looked at it and he said laughing, "You do realise it's probably worthless now?"

"It doesn't matter to me," I replied. "I've read it half a dozen times but I'm never going to sell it!"

Alex thanked me for buying his books and I shook his hand before wishing him a good day and heading over to Jonathan and Ben. We grabbed a few cookies and I bade Laura farewell.

We decided to get something to eat after the book signing, so I quickly dumped the books in my room and we headed out. It was a little after five and the sky was still a deep blue. Although I don't live in Minnesota, I felt sure that the weather was unseasonably warm for the time of year, and I hadn't really packed many light clothes, expecting that the climate would be much cooler. It felt strange to be walking around in shirtsleeves in the American Midwest in April, particularly as I'd read repeatedly over the years that it was perpetually freezing in Minneapolis.

We headed along our usual route, turning right outside the hotel and walking along the buildings that ran alongside it. Electing to find somewhere different to eat than Chuck Wagon Charlie's, we spotted a pizza restaurant opposite the hotel called Pizzaioli at 588 West 78th Street. Before we headed there, I decided to pick up a gift for my wife to thank her for allowing me to undertake this trip. We'd seen a gift store right nearby called Seedlings Gifts and Books at 521 West 78th Street, so we walked there and entered the store.

To our surprise, the store stocked mainly Christian gifts featuring inspirational quotes and passages from the Bible. I spotted a figurine that I knew my wife would like and decided to buy it. Ben spotted some miniature basketballs and joked that Prince may have bought his from here. It's well documented that Prince enjoyed playing the game, and he was reportedly very good at it. Ben reckoned that he must have used smaller equipment as no man that diminutive in stature ought to have been so good at a sport that is predominantly undertaken by players who are taller than the average person. I spoke to the proprietor, a lady named Dee, and her young assistant Emma for a few minutes. I told Dee that I thought Chanhassen was a beautiful city. Dee said that we should visit the Minnesota Landscape Arboretum before we left Chanhassen, and she wrote down directions to it for me and handed me the note, which I put in my wallet. Emma gift-wrapped the figurine I had chosen, and we left the store, heading toward Pizzaioli just across the street.

Entering Pizzaioli at 588 West 78th Street, we saw that the place was empty. Sitting at a table, our server came over and gave us some menus while taking our drinks order. We each ordered pizza and Jonathan and I also ordered some jalapeño bites. Presently our food arrived and we ate and chatted. Tiredness was kicking in terribly now. I still hadn't had a decent night's sleep, and it was beginning to take its toll.

After we finished our meal, it was around 7.00pm. It was still light outside and although the temperature had dropped a little, it was still warm. We headed back to the hotel and decided to turn in for the night as we had an early start in the morning. We were due to begin our last day at *Celebration 2017* at 5.00pm on Sunday, but before that we had the remaining places on our itinerary of Prince-related locations to visit. I'd also added some more places to the list in the last few days, and we now had the last seven to get to before we needed to be at Paisley Park. We didn't know it at the time, but an eighth would be added to the list tomorrow from the unlikeliest of sources, and it would blow our minds. Over our pizzas, we had decided to have another go at trying to find the railroad trestle from *Purple Rain*. We'd already spent an hour driving around Lake Minnetonka before giving up on finding the bridge, but Jonathan had managed to track down some details about the location online and – feeling confident that we could find it this time – we felt it was worth a shot as it was an important spot in the Prince story.

A guy I had spoken to at the Electric Fetus record store a few days before had managed to find the bridge, and had showed me a photo of him standing at it. From the details Jonathan had managed to find, we estimated that it was a sixty mile round trip to get to the spot where the bridge stood. I'd read somewhere a long time ago that it was on private property, so we decided to set off extremely early, as I was anxious to avoid any possible encounters with locals that might not have ended well. I didn't mention it to Jonathan and Ben, but I had visions of a disgruntled landowner wielding his shotgun in our direction for inadvertently trespassing on his property, and I didn't relish the prospect of getting into trouble in a country whose laws I wasn't entirely familiar with.

Retiring to my room, I called my wife and told her about my day. She told me about hers, and I confessed that I was really missing her and the children now. After hanging up, I sent the photos I had taken that day to her, clearing my phone's storage ready for our last full day. I sprawled on the couch and read a few pages of Alex and Laura's new book before drifting off to sleep for a few hours. I awoke at around 10.30pm and showered, then flicked the television on, hit mute, and went to bed.

Waking at 4.00am, I opened the curtains in my room and looked out over the quiet streets like I had done the first night I arrived. Our adventure was nearly over. It was still dark outside, and Chanhassen was asleep. I thought back over what had happened since we got here a week ago, and I really couldn't believe it. It all seemed like a blur. I remember thinking that my friends back home wouldn't believe the things we had seen and done, and I felt thankful that Jonathan and Ben had been here to share it with me. I knew that they were as astounded by it all as I was.

SUNDAY

During breakfast at 6.30am, we spoke to some British girls who were wearing glamorous evening dresses. They had been to a Prince dance-party in town the previous evening which had finished just an hour earlier. We bade them good day and hit the road. It was a beautiful morning and I was very tired, but feeling the sun on my face as I walked out to the car invigorated me somewhat, and I remembered with a smile that we would be seeing the studios at Paisley Park today as part of the tour segment of *Celebration 2017*. This excited me and gave me a much-needed boost of energy.

After working out the route – we had nothing other than a zip code – we pulled out of the Country Inn and Suites parking lot on West 78th Street, and headed south on Market Boulevard opposite the hotel. Passing the Walgreens we had stopped at momentarily the night we had gone to Buffalo Wild Wings, we crossed Arboretum Boulevard and continued south on Market past the AmericInn Chanhassen.

Joining Great Plains Boulevard, we headed southwest and drove for two miles before we crossed Pioneer Trail. Another half a mile flashed by and we turned eastward onto Flying Cloud Drive before taking an immediate right at Bluff Creek. Travelling southeast over flat marshland toward Shakopee, we crossed a bridge with a small marina on it before traversing the Minnesota River on Highway 101. Immediately as we entered Shakopee, we turned westward on 1st Avenue West, travelling alongside the river. Continuing along 1st Avenue we merged with Co Road 69 at North Imports Auto Parts. Passing Shakopee Town Square, we headed further south onto Old Brick Yard Road. Continuing for a few miles, we passed Peter's Pumpkins and Carmen's Corn – which elicited much amusement – and headed through vast areas of rural farmland.

As we drove through the Minnesota countryside, the sky was a gorgeous shade of blue and soft white clouds scudded by, and we listened to Prince tunes on the stereo. The roads were pretty quiet at this time of day – it was still only 7.30am – and as I looked at our surroundings – passing beautiful wooden homesteads, farm buildings, and agricultural machinery in the rolling fields of corn – I felt that this was what the real United States was about. The thrill of knowing we were in the heartland of Middle-America made my heart soar, and I realised with delight that this was the first time I'd seen it first-hand.

Other than an excursion to the Grand Canyon a decade earlier, my previous experiences of the US had been restricted to large urban centres, mainly concentrated on the East and West Coasts of the country. Although I have travelled countrywide in America, I had always flown, and consequently I only saw the cities I had been staying in. The freedom the car had given us on this trip was a joy, and I resolved to personally thank Bill – a friend from back in the UK – who had suggested hiring an automobile rather than using public transport and cabs, which had originally been the plan. Looking back, it's patently clear that we wouldn't have seen everything that way.

We turned right onto West 150th Street and at the Minnesota Valley Garden Center, we joined Johnson Memorial Drive and headed toward the small city of Jordan – population approximately 5000 – in Scott County. Driving through the town, we picked up Highway 169. A few miles out of Jordan, we passed the bright yellow building of Minnesota's Largest Candy Store. The picket fence surrounding the store was painted yellow too. Continuing southwest, we drove through the city of Belle Plaine, before heading out into the countryside and across miles of arable farmland once more. We were now heading due south, and I realised we were approaching our destination with just a couple more miles to go until we were at the railroad trestle, and the spot where the 'Take Me With U' segment of the *Purple Rain* movie was shot.

We approached 280th Street West and turned right onto it. As we reached the left bend that took us toward the Ney Nature Center on our left, Jonathan hit play on the song that features in this part of *Purple Rain*, and set the video option on his phone to record. We drove towards Henderson Station Road and the bridge – recreating the moment for ourselves – some thirty-four years later. As 'Take Me With U' played and we wound our way through wooded lanes with the sunlight filtering through the trees on this peaceful Sunday morning, it was not hard to see why this gorgeous spot was chosen for the movie.

Suddenly a right turn appeared out of nowhere. I had to hit the brakes sharply to avoid missing it, and I almost turned the car back on ourselves before heading north onto Henderson Station Road. I say 'road', it was more of a dirt track the width of two cars. We had no idea how long the road was – or where the bridge was located – so I drove slowly along the unmarked road at no more than twenty miles per hour. Travelling parallel to the rail track, we followed the path of the Minnesota River. Our eyes were everywhere as we scanned our surroundings for the spot from *Purple Rain*.

At around fifteen hundred metres, we suddenly saw the location we were looking for. There on the left – in a clearing through the trees – we spotted the railway trestle that Prince parks his motorcycle at in the movie. It was rusty and was made from riveted girders. The bridge was set back from the roadside fifty feet and spanned the marshland at the edge of the Minnesota River which stretched out beyond it. Passing the spot – we saw it a little too late to pull up – I planned to turn the car around at a suitable point and go back so we could get out for a closer look.

I drove a little further – onto Chatfield Drive – and on our right there was a slightly sinister dilapidated old wooden house. It had an old '70's Cadillac – or some similar automobile – rotting in the yard, and we decided it probably wasn't safe for us to hang around too long. I carried on past the house and at the next available opportunity, I turned the car around and headed back the way we had just came. As we drew parallel with the rusty wrought–iron bridge, I stopped the car and switched off the engine.

We got out of the car and the air was absolutely silent. It was one of those gorgeous spring mornings where the air is crisp but the temperature is agreeable. I looked at my watch. It was just before eight in the morning. Looking around, I was pretty sure that I'd parked the car at the exact place where Prince turns his motorcycle off the track and rides under the bridge in the movie. I searched online for a still of Prince at the spot but – somewhat unsurprisingly – I didn't have a signal on my phone. Jonathan did though, and he quickly found one. As I had suspected, we were on the same spot. Save for the trestle being rustier than in 1983 – when *Purple Rain* was shot – the picturesque location was almost exactly the same. The grass was a bit greener in the movie – it was April now after all – but the site was largely unchanged. We laughed and I imagined what this place must have looked like all those years ago, with a film crew watching on as a local musical superstar made a little film that would go on to win him an Oscar and become one of the most famous rock movies of all time. I recalled how many times I had watched *Purple Rain* throughout my life – it must be in the dozens, as I viewed it incessantly as a teenager – and it felt surreal to be standing at the spot I had first seen as a fourteen year old boy. Jonathan, Ben and I gleefully took photos of each other in front of the bridge, under the bridge, and alongside the bridge. I looked out across the Minnesota River and it was beautiful, just so serene. I wished I could just sit there all day. None of us could believe we had actually found this place. It was so far off the beaten track you could drive around for a day and not find it. *Especially if you're not even in the right part of Minnesota.* As we stood on the dirt track, we laughed about that.

We spent half an hour on Henderson Station Road taking photographs of the iconic little bridge before we decided to head back to civilisation, and our next stop on my itinerary. With a sigh, I said goodbye to the famous spot in Prince's story, and got in the car. Jonathan sets the GPS for Dupont Avenue South near Uptown in northeast Minneapolis. It was a forty mile drive, and it was still only 8.30am. This location was the spot that Chris Moon's studio – originally on Stevens Avenue South, the little house we had visited a few days ago – moved to as it expanded. Housed in a commercial building that offered a better environment in which to record, Prince worked there once he had established his skills. Selecting the *Purple Rain* soundtrack on Ben's mp3 player in the car, we set off.

We travelled back to Chanhassen the way we came. The journey took forty minutes. From our hotel we followed the route we had taken on Friday to Calhoun Square in Uptown, and this time I drove past the building on West Lake Street that was immortalised in the Prince tune of the same name. Turning left onto Emerson Avenue South two blocks later – just before the entrance to the Arby's restaurant on our right – we drove a further two blocks until we reached the Elan Uptown Apartments on our right. From there, we turned right onto West 28th Street and then effectively doubled back on ourselves, turning right again onto Dupont Avenue South.

We were looking for 2828 Dupont Avenue South, but the GPS positioned our destination outside the opposite side of the Elan building. Confused, we got out of the car and walked to the building's entrance, which was up a flight of concrete steps. Checking the apartment numbers, we found that they didn't correspond with the address we were looking for. On the opposite side of the road – behind us – is an almost identical building. Again, it had concrete steps leading up through the building's courtyard. Number 2828 corresponded with this apartment block. We walked through the open air courtyard to the other side of the building. We passed a ground floor apartment that was numbered 2828. The building we were looking for wasn't an apartment. It was a large red single storey building, so we knew this wasn't it. Coming out of the complex on the other side of the building, we found ourselves on a street called Colfax Avenue South. We consulted the internet, and were informed that the property we were looking for is next to an auto impound yard. The yard was supposedly on Colfax. There was no sign of an auto impound. We were in a residential area. Walking back through the courtyard to the car, we got in and drove around the perimeter of both apartment buildings a few times looking for something that might give us a clue, but it was no use. We were drawing a complete blank. Suddenly, we spotted a tiny parking lot with cars that looked like they may have been impounded. We figured that we must be in the right place. Returning to the spot that the GPS instructed us was the correct location for 2828 Dupont Avenue South, we concluded that the building that once housed Moon Sound must no longer be standing. We got out of the car again – and with not a lot else to go on – we took photos of each other sitting on the concrete steps leading up to the current building's entrance.

Feeling slightly disappointed, we decided to move on to the next location, and I turned the car east onto West 28th Street again and drove four blocks before we spotted a Subway restaurant on the corner of West 28th and Lyndale Avenue South. Deciding we should hydrate, I swung the car into the parking lot and we went inside. We ordered drinks and Jonathan consulted his phone in another effort to locate 2828 Dupont Avenue South. We were still not sure that we had found the right place. Again, he found nothing that really helped us.

"Never mind," I said. "We still have a few more to get to."

As we sat in the restaurant, I looked over my shoulder and saw a sign on the front of a building with the words 'Lyndale Ave' on it.

"Rudolphs Bar-B-Que must be near here," said Jonathan.

It was our next stop. We asked the restaurant staff if they knew where Rudolphs was but they told us they were not sure. Jonathan checked the address. It was at 1933 Lyndale Avenue South. The number on the building outside was in the 2700s. Figuring it was north from here, we headed out and jumped in the car. Travelling north along Lyndale Avenue, we passed Treehouse Records at 2557 Lyndale on the corner of West 26th Street, and six blocks up on the right hand side of the road, we spotted Rudolphs on the corner of West Franklin Avenue.

Rudolphs Bar-B-Que is an upscale-casual bar serving comfort food and barbecue classics. The building is inspired by its namesake, the 1920s actor Rudolph Valentino. Opened in 1975 by Jack Theros as an alternative to the downmarket barbecue joints that were prevalent in Minnesota at the time, Rudolph's gave diners in Minneapolis a touch of class. The restaurant is now run by Jack's son, Charlie.

Prince was a frequent customer at Rudolphs – particularly in the '80s – and he was always given a table toward the back of the bar where he could eat in privacy. He would often go to Rudolphs with band members if they had been rehearsing. Sometimes, he just dined alone.

I parked the car just before Harriet Avenue on Franklin, and we walked back to the restaurant on the corner. It is a fabulous looking building. Its design is rooted firmly in the '70s and painted a rustic orange and cream, and it features a picture of Valentino above the door. We stood across the street and took photos of the exterior, before crossing and standing in the doorway for further photo opportunities. As I stood in the entrance, I suddenly heard music coming from inside. Looking at my watch, I saw that it was just after 10.00am. Jonathan and Ben were on the opposite side of the street.

"I think it's open," I shouted, and they came over to the door. I opened it, and we walked inside.

Rudolphs looked exactly how I imagined it would. It had a beautiful black and white tiled floor and a large island bar in the middle of the room. Behind the counter, female servers were hard at work getting ready for the day's customers. The place was completely empty. I figured that people must like their barbecue a little later in the day. One of the girls behind the bar approached me.

"Good morning," she said, "Welcome to Rudolphs. Would you guys like a table?"

I said that we were fine, and we were only stopping by as we were on a Prince pilgrimage around Minneapolis, and that we hadn't expected Rudolphs to be open this early on a Sunday morning. Upon hearing my accent she asked if we were British. I said that we were, and she motioned for us to follow her, saying, "You need to come with me."

We followed her toward the back of the bar, and on the right hand side we stopped at a booth where two men were sitting.

"These are my friends from England," she said to them. "Guys, this is Charlie and Ken."

Charlie Theros introduced himself and told us that he was the proprietor of Rudolphs. Ken was his friend. Both men looked to be in their mid-fifties. We shook hands and they asked why we were there. We told him that we were Prince *fam*. To our utter amazement, Charlie immediately recognised our accents, right down to the region we are from. I asked him how he knew, and he told us that he followed British soccer and had heard the 'Geordie' accent that is common near where I live. He then mentioned Middlesbrough's football team and I congratulated him on his sound – not to mention surprising – knowledge of North East English dialects.

We talked about our itinerary and *Celebration 2017*, and he asked if we wanted to hear some anecdotes about Prince. We excitedly said that we would, and Charlie told us that Prince had been a regular visitor.

"We always snuck him in through the back door," he said. "And he always left the same way."

I glanced back down the bar and near the door we had walked in was a huge *Purple Rain* poster.

Charlie continued. "Once, Janet Jackson was in town on a day off from recording her *Rhythm Nation* album with Jimmy Jam and Terry Lewis, and Prince threw a surprise party for her here. The place was closed to the public and we had a ton of celebrities turn up in a line of limos that went halfway down the street."

I asked if Charlie had ever spoken to Prince.

"Of course," he said. "Many times. He was a really great guy, down to earth and very courteous. We were always very protective of him too. He was a local hero."

Ken – who until now had been sitting quietly while Charlie talked – asked us where else we had left to visit, and we told them our plans for the rest of the day. I mentioned that we weren't sure if we had found the right place we were looking for at Dupont Avenue South. I told him that it was a studio Prince had recorded at early in his career. I also said that Prince had first recorded at Moon Sound's first address in the single family home on Stevens Avenue. The auto impound also came up in the conversation.

Ken raised his eyebrows, and said that the only impound he knew of was the Minneapolis Impound Lot about a mile north of Rudolphs in the Harrison district of town. We checked online, and found that the pound was on Colfax Avenue *North*. We'd been on Colfax Avenue *South*. We said we'd check it out.

Ken looked at Charlie. "Shall I tell them?" he asked.

Charlie said, "Sure," and Ken then asked us a question that I didn't know the answer to.

"Do you know where else Prince recorded in the early days?" he asked.

I replied that I wasn't sure.

Ken went on, "Have you heard of 430 Oak Grove Street?"

I replied that I hadn't.

"No one really has," said Ken smiling. "It's not well known about, but it's just round the corner. Do you want to go?"

I looked at Jonathan and Ben. None of us had heard of Oak Grove Street.

"How do you know he recorded there?" I asked.

"I knew Prince," he said. "We were friends until High School. After that, I followed his career quite closely."

We looked at him incredulously, and he laughed and said that Prince had always given him free tickets when he was playing in town. Ken told us how Prince had recorded at the first floor offices of his then-manager Owen Husney on Oak Grove Street in 1977. Known as the *Loring Park Sessions*, the tracks Prince recorded – long instrumental funk jams that didn't get as far as being titled – showcased his virtuosity as a musician, but belied his skills as a songwriter.

After I got home from the US, I investigated further and found that the day after we spoke to Charlie and Ken at Rudolphs, Prince's first manager Owen Husney and André Cymone – his childhood friend and bandmate – had unveiled a plaque inside the building at 430 Oak Grove Street to mark the importance of the site in Prince's musical development. The event made the local newspapers. I guess it's not a secret anymore, huh, Ken? Since then, I have also acquired a copy of the recordings the young Prince made there. They are interesting to hear but do not give a true indication of what was to come in his work.

Thanking Ken for his offer to take us to Oak Grove Street, I told him that we had a car and GPS and we would find our own way there without interrupting his day any further. We had our photos taken with Charlie and Ken by the girl who had introduced us to them – she took several photos with my phone and then again with Charlie's – and we shook hands with them before heading back to the car.

Excited, we looked up Oak Grove Street, and punched the address details into the GPS. It was four minutes away. I couldn't believe it. We'd just discovered an important part of the Prince legend that we'd never heard of before.

Situated between The Woman's Club of Minneapolis and Saint Mark's Episcopal Church, the apartment block at 430 Oak Grove Street in Loring Park is an imposing white stone building with dark grey window frames. With a huge arched entrance, the northwest facing facade is a grand sight. The edifice sits right on the edge of the park and has changed a lot since the days when Owen Husney rented an office there - it is now a residential apartment block – but since returning from Minneapolis, I have discovered that it is instrumental in Prince's story. It was here that Prince first met Bobby Z – the future Revolution drummer who I had walked into Paisley Park with on Friday. 430 Oak Grove Street is also the place where Chris Moon – Prince's first serious collaborator at Moon Sound and co-writer of his first single, 'Soft and Wet' – introduced the young musician to Owen, the man who helped him to get a record deal, setting him on the road to superstardom.

Heading east on West Franklin Avenue, we turned left onto Pillsbury Avenue South then left again onto Groveland Avenue. After a third of a mile, I turned the car right onto Clifton Place and at the end of the road – directly facing us – was the old office of Prince's first manager. I pulled the car over across the street from 430 Oak Grove Street. Realising we had quite a few places left to get to today, we quickly took some photos before continuing on our way.

As we headed northwest, Jonathan searched online for the Minneapolis Impound Lot on Colfax Avenue North. Figuring we should check it out just to be sure that we were at the right place on Dupont Avenue South earlier when we were trying to locate the old Moon Sound spot, I drove north on Hennepin Avenue. Joining Lyndale Avenue South, we branched left at Hawthorne Avenue West and followed the North Loop onto East Lyndale Avenue North. From there we headed east on Glenwood Avenue. On Glenwood, we passed an audio gear salesroom called HiFi Sound, and I told Jonathan to grab a photo of it for a friend back home in the UK who owns a high-end audio equipment shop with the same name. Turning left onto Colfax Avenue North, we drove to the end of the street and arrived at the impound lot. Checking the old photo of the red single storey building Moon Sound occupied, we spent the next twenty minutes driving around the streets surrounding the lot looking for it. Sadly, we found no sign of the building. Finally admitting defeat for good, we agreed that we should move on – we'd now spent ninety minutes looking for the place – so we headed off to our next port of call. I found out when I got back to the UK that the building was torn down a few years ago, and what was built on the site? You guessed it. The apartment block we had stopped at earlier that morning. We had been at the right place after all.

Susannah Melvoin is the twin sister of The Revolution's Wendy. Joining the expanded line-up of the band in 1986, Susannah performed backing vocals on the *Parade* album from the same year. She also played keyboards and sang in Prince protégés The Family during their short existence. The Prince-penned 'Nothing Compares 2 U' – later a worldwide smash hit for Sinead O'Connor – was reportedly written about Susannah, who was engaged to Prince for a time in the '80s. We'd seen Susannah at Paisley Park on Friday performing with The Revolution. Today, she was appearing at the Electric Fetus record store, and we were on our way there. Mark had told us that he would see us there when he had left us the previous afternoon.

Arriving at Electric Fetus at 11.00am, we had thirty minutes before Susannah was due to appear. As we entered the building, Jonathan spotted that the store had a few copies of the *Piano & A Microphone Tour* programme on sale for twenty five dollars. They were limited to one per customer so we each picked one up. It now sells for ten times that. As we'd expected, the queue to meet Susannah was huge, so the store was operating a ticket system to ensure the event would remain civilised. We checked our bags – store policy – and I took a ticket. It was number forty-four. As I did so, I read the notice board next to the desk that Susannah would be sitting at. It said that she would be unveiling the proposed artwork she had designed for an aborted Prince album named *Dream Factory* from the '80s. I was excited by this news.

To pass the time before Susannah arrived, I browsed the second-hand vinyl section. Not finding anything I wanted after five minutes, I wandered over to the end of the line and – checking my number against the last person there – I made my way to my position in the procession that snaked around the racks of records toward the desk. People graciously made room for me, and the atmosphere was good-natured as *fam* chatted excitedly to each other. I discovered that I was next to a guy from London so we began making small talk. He was called Rob, and was there alone. Rob mistakenly thought I was from Newcastle – a "Geordie" – so I corrected him, laughing. We chatted for a few minutes about *Celebration 2017* and suddenly, Susannah was right there.

Wearing ubiquitous rock star shades, Susannah Melvoin – one time fiancée of Prince – sported a form-fitting black padded nylon jacket and skin-tight black jeans that were faded slightly, and her tousled hair was casually tied up with stray strands hanging down over her face. She looked sensational. Her outfit was finished with a green patterned scarf and taupe ankle boots.

As Susannah appeared, a cheer went up from the crowd and she stood waving and smiling to everyone before sitting at the desk. The artwork for the planned album cover Susannah was about to share with us was sitting on an easel next to her with a black cover draped over it. Without warning, an assistant removed the cloth and we strained to get a glimpse of the artwork for the *Dream Factory* album.

Dream Factory is an unreleased LP by Prince with input on several numbers from The Revolution. Recorded over several years, it was pencilled in for release in 1986 but was ultimately shelved during the dissolution of the band that year. Many of the tracks scheduled for *Dream Factory* were then incorporated into a proposed triple album named *Crystal Ball*. Warner Brothers – Prince's label at the time – balked at a three LP set. Feeling that he was saturating the market with too much new material – and the cost of producing a triple LP being prohibitively expensive – they vetoed the release.

Crystal Ball was eventually pared down to a double album – retitled *Sign o' the Times* – and released in March 1987. *Sign o' the Times* showcases the breadth of Prince's staggering musical ability and displays his mastery over a multitude of styles and genres. The album includes several tracks performed by 'Camille'

– Prince's alter-ego of the time – which featured the strangely distorted vocals with altered pitch that Prince's engineer Susan Rogers had inadvertently created. *Sign o' the Times* went on to achieve huge critical acclaim and is now widely regarded as one of the greatest albums of all time. Prince, however, was allegedly unsatisfied with *Sign o' the Times* as he felt his original artistic vision for *Dream Factory* had been compromised somewhat. *Sign o' the Times* includes the track 'Starfish & Coffee' co-written by Susannah Melvoin.

Crystal Ball was eventually released in 1998, but by this point had evolved from the original album Prince had envisaged in '86 into a triple CD compilation of previously bootlegged material. A small number of the original *Dream Factory* songs remained intact – 'Sexual Suicide', 'Last Heart', 'Movie Star', 'Crystal Ball', and the title track – and saw their first official release on this set.

The queue of *fam* in the Electric Fetus record store slowly made its way forward as each person met Susannah and posed for pictures with her and the artwork for *Dream Factory*. As we neared the front of the queue, I spotted a guy in a baseball cap walking around behind Susannah, looking at records and CDs. He was quiet and alone. Nobody else spotted him but I recognised him immediately and I was thrilled that he was there.

While I had been waiting my turn to meet Susannah, I had been studying the proposed cover for the aborted album. Roughly the size of an LP sleeve, it is a colour pencil sketch depicting a time-warp flash. The figure of a woman – presumably Susannah herself – stands at an open door. She is wearing a gold backless dress – tied with a purple bow – and matching gold shoes. Her hand is at her mouth as she looks out toward the *Dream Factory* beyond, signified by the sun, a crescent moon, stars, coloured balloons, and a rainbow. The album cover is bordered in purple and features little red hearts and wilting flowers of many colours. Interestingly, there is no mention of Prince or The Revolution on the sleeve. Instead, it is attributed to 'The Flesh'.

The Flesh was a group proposed by Prince in 1986 that did not come to full fruition. Primarily, the band comprised of Prince and his saxophonist Eric Leeds, with contributions from members of The Revolution. Eric was also a member of 1985 Prince protégés The Family, along with Susannah. Although recordings made by The Flesh are believed to exist, none have been released officially and the band was seen as a precursor to the jazz-rock group named Madhouse that Prince and Eric formed a short time later. Madhouse released two official albums of instrumental music – the first of Prince's career – in 1987 and 1988. The man in the baseball cap who I had just recognised in Electric Fetus was Eric Leeds.

Rob – the guy in front of me in the queue – asked if I would take his picture when he got his moment with Susannah and handed me his phone. He sat with Prince's ex-fiancée for a moment and I deftly grabbed a dozen photos of him with her from different angles. He came back to me with a broad grin on his face and thanked me before moving to one side. I asked Jonathan to take some photos of me with Susannah. I sat next to her and we hugged. I told her how much I had enjoyed The Revolution's set at Paisley Park and her surprise appearance there, and she laughed and said thanks. She asked if I was from England and I told her I was. We posed for a photo next to the artwork for *Dream Factory* and then I moved to the side for Jonathan, and I took pictures of him with Susannah on his phone.

Walking behind Susannah, I crossed to the other side of the queue and approached Eric Leeds. He was looking on quietly as *fam* met her, and I was the only person to approach him.

"Hi, Eric," I said.

He looked at me, seemingly surprised to be recognised.

"Hi," he said back, and we shook hands. Dressed casually, he cut an unassuming figure in the record store, and was clearly happy for Susannah to have the limelight.

Eric Leeds was Prince's saxophonist for the best part of twenty years. Introduced to Prince shortly after the *Purple Rain Tour* by his brother Alan – who was Prince's tour manager – Eric joined The Family in 1985 before being incorporated into the expanded line-up of The Revolution in '86, playing on the *Parade*

Tour from that year. He continued to work with Prince off and on for the next two decades as well as releasing his own albums on Paisley Park Records. In 2009, The Family reformed under the name fDeluxe. They have released three albums so far. Eric is now working on a new project with Paul Peterson – another former member of The Family – named LP Music.

I thanked Eric for his work with Prince and told him that I'm a jazz nut who owns pretty much all of his output. He smiled and thanked me, and I told him that it had been over thirty years since I first saw him. He laughed and said that it all seemed like yesterday. I asked if I could take a photo with him, and he graciously granted me permission to do so. I grabbed a few photos in quick succession – I always do this – and shook his hand once more before saying goodbye. He thanked me again and I moved over to Jonathan who was waiting for Ben, who was sitting with Susannah Melvoin. I told him that I'd just met Eric. Jonathan told me that Susannah liked his name, and they spoke about her late brother – also named Jonathan – and his work with the band Smashing Pumpkins. As we took photos of Ben, Susannah suddenly introduced Eric Leeds to the crowd and he walked over, waving to everyone before giving her a hug.

We spent a few minutes watching Susannah meet more *fam* and decided it was time for us to leave. Sadly, there was still no sign of Mark. Foolishly, I had omitted to get his cell phone number so I wasn't even able to call him while we were at Electric Fetus. We had a few more spots to get to before meeting him for day four at *Celebration 2017* in Paisley Park, and I mentioned to Jonathan and Ben that he may still get to the Electric Fetus in time to meet Susannah. We knew Mark would be tired. He had attended the Prince-themed dance-party in Downtown the previous night – where the girls we had spoken to during breakfast that morning had been – but Jonathan, Ben and I had decided against going, in order to get an early start on the long drive to the *Purple Rain* railway bridge I had undertaken earlier.

As we left, I noted that the *Piano & A Microphone Tour* books had now sold out. The guy behind the counter had marked our hands with permanent marker when we had picked up our copies which was clearly a shrewd move designed to combat people surreptitiously purchasing additional copies of the book to sell on for a profit. As a result I had been unable to procure a copy for Mark.

It was now 12.30pm. We headed through the crowds, picked up our checked bags, and exited the record store. The posters on the door were still there, promoting the in-store appearance of Susannah that we had just left, and the CD signing the following day by Ida Nielsen – bassist with Prince's final band 3rdeyegirl. Ben – who is a keen bassist and huge fan of Ida's – was dismayed that we would not be able to attend. We were due to fly from Minneapolis St-Paul to Charles de Gaulle Airport in Paris on the first connecting flight of our journey home to the UK the following afternoon at the same time that Ida would be at the Electric Fetus. With a sigh, Ben resigned himself to the fact that he wouldn't be meeting his hero and we consoled him before heading off to our next stop.

We now had four hours before we were back at Paisley Park for our final day at *Celebration 2017* and there were three locations left for us to find. Starting the car, Jonathan set the GPS and hit the shuffle option on the stereo. The opening title track from Prince's 1985 album *Around the World in a Day* began. Jonathan and I looked at each other in amazement. It was a fortuitous moment. Susannah Melvoin's late brother Jonathan plays on the track. We bid farewell to Prince's local record store and hit the road.

Situated on Lake Riley a few miles south of Chanhassen, sits Kiowa Trail. Many of the waterfront homes there are luxurious and prices can run into the hundreds of thousands of dollars. It was here that Prince moved into the famous 'Purple House' at 9401 Kiowa Trail in the winter of 1980. The exterior of the two-storey ranch-style split level house was originally cream coloured, but Prince had it painted purple upon purchasing it. Setting up a 16-track home studio on the ground floor – in what was formerly a family room to the right of the front door – Prince installed the latest equipment, and upstairs in the living room, a piano was wired directly to the studio so Prince could record from it whenever the mood struck him. In a move possibly designed to make the studio as accessible as possible at any hour of the day or night, Prince also set up a master bedroom on the ground floor opposite the studio.

In 1982, the studio was upgraded to a 24-channel facility, and it was at the 'Purple House' that many of Prince's most beloved numbers such as '1999' and 'Raspberry Beret' were initially tracked. In addition, many numbers by protégés The Time, Apollonia 6, and Vanity 6 were also recorded at this address. Prince lived in the home on Kiowa Trail until early 1985, moving to 7141 Galpin Boulevard – site of the 'Yellow House' five miles northwest from this spot – before finally taking up residency in his custom-built Paisley Park complex after its construction was completed in 1988. After Prince left 9401 Kiowa Trail, his father John L Nelson subsequently moved into the property, where he remained until his death in 2001.

Sadly, the house is no longer there. Prince had it torn down in March 2003, but retained ownership of the land the 'Purple House' had sat on until his passing in April 2016. The large black steel gate is still there though, marking the location of Prince's former home, and it was to this site – twenty miles from the Electric Fetus record store – that we now travelled.

Heading south from the Minneapolis Convention Center on I-35W, we drove for six miles before turning right at Nicolett Park and following the MN-62 through Edina for a further six, passing Bredesen Park and heading south on US 212-W. Picking up Great Plains Boulevard, we headed south again for a mile or so, before reaching Kiowa Trail on the left.

Three hundred feet up the quiet lane on the right hand side of Kiowa Trail and partially hidden through the trees – so much so that we actually missed it and sailed straight past – was the gate to Prince's former home. Turning the car around, I parked right outside. We got out and took a closer look.

There were two female Prince *fam* standing by the gate. Speaking to them, we found that they were from the Netherlands. I asked if they would like me to take their photo in front of the gate, and accepting my offer they posed outside the entrance to the site where the 'Purple House' once stood. Returning the favour, they took photos of me, Jonathan, and Ben standing in front of the gate too.

On the right side of the black steel gate – at head height – a stylised steel heart denoting 'love' was attached to the gate. It measured about three feet across. On the left side was a similarly proportioned steel 'peace' symbol, famously designed by British artist Gerald Holtom for the Campaign for Nuclear Disarmament movement in 1958. The tree-lined drive beyond the gate swept round to the left where the house had been, and it was a beautiful serene spot. As we stood outside the gate, another car pulled up and a group of Prince *fam* we recognised from our hotel climbed out. They walked over to the gate and snapped each other in front of it. We talked about the next spot we were going to, and they told us that they had just come from there. It was the site of another home that Prince owned – his last before moving to Paisley Park – and we said goodbye and headed back to the car. Punching the address into the GPS, we saw that the next house was just a short drive from where we were sitting. It struck me that Prince didn't move very far between his last three homes. All are situated in Chanhassen. He clearly loved it there.

I swung the car around and travelled back the way we came. Heading north on Great Plains Boulevard, we passed Bandimere Heights Park on our right and skirted Lake Susan, heading back into Chanhassen. From there, we headed west on Arboretum Boulevard – passing Paisley Park on our left – before travelling half a mile further then turning right onto Galpin Boulevard. Travelling half a mile again along Galpin, we reached a bulk water filling station on the right side of the road. It was one of two for public use in Chanhassen. The gate to Prince's next home was just before you get to it. Pulling the car over at the filling station, we got out and walked to the gate of Prince's famous 'Yellow House' at 7141 Galpin Boulevard.

In late 1985, Prince moved into the three storey yellow mansion appropriately known as the 'Yellow House'. Situated on thirty acres of land, the new property afforded Prince the opportunity to build a state-of-the-art recording studio large enough to house an entire band set-up. Like the house on Kiowa Trail, the studio was situated downstairs and a piano – this one painted purple – sat in an upstairs living room and was wired to the studio below. Although Prince acquired the property just before Christmas of 1985, he didn't actually use the studio until several months later – March '86 – as he was recording at the famous Sunset Sound studios in Hollywood, California. Prince and Eric Leeds' two Madhouse studio albums were recorded at the 'Yellow House' on Galpin Boulevard, and the first song ever committed to tape there was 'The Ballad of Dorothy Parker' from the 1987 *Sign o' the Times* album.

The grounds featured a swimming pool, which was utilised as the location for the shooting of the 'Gangster Glam' promotional video in 1991. Prince protégée Jill Jones also recorded portions of her debut self-titled album at Galpin Boulevard. Her album – released in 1987 – is generally regarded as one of the best Prince side-projects. Jill – an early girlfriend of Prince's who performed backing vocals on the title track and 'Lady Cab Driver' from 1982's *1999* album – plays the blonde waitress, also named Jill, in *Purple Rain*. As with the 'Purple House' on Kiowa Trail, the 'Yellow House' at 7141 Galpin Boulevard is no longer standing. Prince had it razed in 2005, again maintaining ownership of the land thereafter.

Reaching the gate to the 'Yellow House', we could see that we were not alone. To the left of the gate was a large security building with blacked-out windows – long abandoned – and standing next to it were two American women who were in their forties. To our surprise, they were drinking cans of beer. It was just before 2.00pm in the afternoon. Shocked to see us approach them, they hid their drinks – somewhat unsuccessfully – and started taking photos of the gate.

I asked if they would like me to take one of both of them, and they politely declined. They took some of us though, and we began chatting.

One of the women was called Cindy. She was from Texas. The other lady was Monica. She was from North Carolina. One of us – I can't remember who – cracked a funny and mentioned 'Cindy C', a track from Prince's infamous December 1987 LP, *The Black Album*.

Recorded as party music for a birthday bash planned for Sheila E and shelved by Prince himself at the last minute, *The Black Album* – which actually has no official title and is housed in a plain black sleeve – is the most bootlegged album in history. It received an extremely limited official release in November 1994 and was deleted again after just a month on sale.

Cindy – either not getting the reference or just not finding it amusing – didn't laugh. Sensing an extremely awkward moment was about to unfold, I quickly asked if they were long time Prince *fam*.

"Yes," said Cindy. "In fact, I know him."

Monica just smiled at us. Apart from declining our offer to take their photo, she didn't speak the entire time we were there.

"You knew him?" I asked, looking at Jonathan and Ben.

"Sure," said Cindy. "I talk to him all the time." She was speaking in the present tense.

Again, I looked at my travelling companions.

Cindy continued talking. "I'm a psychic medium. I communicate with Prince every day. He tells me everything. Isn't that right, Monica?"

Monica nodded and smiled.

"I'm also a Witch," continued Cindy, "and Monica is my spiritual companion."

We were lost for words and looked at her blankly.

Cindy told us that Prince often took her shopping – I almost started laughing at this – and she said that earlier, they had gone to the Mall Of America in Minneapolis for Monica to buy a gift for her sister back home.

"Monica wanted to spend fifty dollars," said Cindy, "but Prince made her spend sixty-six dollars. He's a scamp." She laughed at this, and thankful for the opportunity to do so, we laughed too.

With that, Cindy said that they must be going and we said goodbye to them both. She told us to find her on social media, but failed to give us her surname. We didn't ask for it and hung around at the gate of 7141 Galpin Boulevard for a few minutes, until Cindy and Monica were out of sight. Then we looked at each other, and laughed like crazy. As we walked back to the car, I noted that it was approaching 2.00pm. We were due at Paisley Park at 5.00pm. We had two locations left to find.

Heading back to Chanhassen, we went past our hotel heading east and picked up West 78th Street. Passing Goodwill Chanhassen and heading into Eden Prairie, we turned right at Mitchell Road and drove past the Police Department headquarters. From there we turned left onto Anderson Lakes Parkway and followed the road southwest for one and a half miles, before turning right onto Flying Cloud Drive. We followed the road for four miles – deviating onto Bryant Lake Drive at Valley View Road and then turning right onto Shady Oak Road before rejoining Flying Cloud Drive – and we reached our destination.

In 1983, the shooting of *Purple Rain* took place from November through December at several locations throughout Minneapolis and the surrounding area. A storage space at 6472 Flying Cloud Drive was one of the spots used at the time. Approximately twenty-five scenes were filmed here from November 21st to 25th – either side of Thanksgiving that year – including many of the segments of the movie that took place in the basement bedroom and home of Prince's character 'The Kid'. Morris' bathroom scene was also shot here. The facility also doubled as a dance rehearsal space where the cast of *Purple Rain* were put through their paces in preparation for the musical sequences in the film. The building – like many of the locations we had visited today –

no longer exists at the spot where the film crew worked all those years ago. A new building has now been erected there – housing a business that provides medical equipment – and we drove into the parking lot – which was next to a small pond – and took a few photos of our surroundings before we moved on.

Flying Cloud Drive also had another site connected to *Purple Rain*, but this time it was not related to the movie. 9025 Flying Cloud Drive was the site of a rehearsal space Prince used to record band performances by The Revolution in 1984, while preparing for the massive *Purple Rain Tour*. The warehouse on the site was also used as a recording studio, and initial tracking for much of the 1985 *Around the World in a Day* album, which was recorded throughout the previous year, was done there. The facility was purchased by Prince and converted into a usable space, but problems with sound leakage meant the building wasn't ideal, and in the spring of 1985 it was torn down. Planning for a larger creative space on the site began – it even got as far as construction drawings being submitted – but the envisaged recording facility never reached fruition. Ultimately deeming the site unsuitable due to its limited size, and facing restrictions from Eden Prairie building regulators, the proposed location for what would become the famous Paisley Park complex was switched to its present day site at Audubon Road in Chanhassen, and in a time and money saving exercise, the plans that had already been drawn up were incorporated into the new building.

We left Flying Cloud Drive and had one final destination to find. It was the last location connected to Prince that we would visit on our trip to Minnesota. Like the last two stops, it was a rehearsal space where the building no longer existed.

The Warehouse was a former pet food storage facility located in the St Louis Park district of Minneapolis. Converted into a rehearsal space and used by the cast of *Purple Rain* as a base for acting and dance classes in preparation for the movie, the building at 6651 Highway 7 was also used as a recording studio. A version of 'Let's Go Crazy' – the opening track of the *Purple Rain* soundtrack album – was recorded there, but – like the building at 9025 Flying Cloud Drive – the property wasn't particularly suited to recording, and there were problems with sound leakage. In fact, the recording console didn't even have a separate booth.

We planned to visit the Warehouse before heading back to our hotel in Chanhassen and then meeting Mark at Paisley Park. Jonathan entered the address details into the GPS and we set off. After a short while on the road, we hit a blockade. The road we needed to take was completely closed. Turning the car around, I drove away from the roadblock and planned to find an alternative route. After five minutes of driving without following any particular route, I stopped the car and we entered the details of the Warehouse address again. Unfortunately, the GPS sent us back to the same spot – albeit via a different set of roads – and we hit the roadblock again. We had no other means of finding out another route. It was now after 3.00pm.

"What do you want to do?" I asked Jonathan and Ben. "Should we give up and head back to the hotel?"

Agreeing that we didn't have much time to continue looking for a way to get to St Louis Park, we decided to head back to Chanhassen. We were slightly disappointed to have not reached the final spot on our itinerary, but we were in good spirits nonetheless. *Celebration 2017* was only a few hours away, and today was the day that we would finally be touring the building. It was one of the parts of the trip that we had been looking forward to the most. In fact, I was so excited about the tour that I had actually booked us onto a second one the following day – at 10.30am – just before we left Minneapolis for home.

Arriving at our hotel we just had time to freshen up before heading back out to Paisley Park. I phoned my wife and told her what I had been doing that day. I also sent her the photos I had taken, and I met Jonathan and Ben in the hotel lobby to drive back to Paisley Park.

I parked in our usual spot on Park Road at the back of Paisley Park, and we waited for Mark to arrive. As he did so, another car parked right behind his. It was a bright yellow Corvette Z51. Bruce – the American guy I had seen at the merchandise stall buying the three Cloud guitars on the first day we had been inside Paisley Park – climbed out of the sports car. As I looked at him, I remembered that he had also been onstage during The Time's set yesterday. He greeted us with a smile and we shook hands, and Mark said that he had met Bruce at the Prince dance-party the previous evening. We looked at Bruce's car for a minute and I noticed that the doors had the faint outline of Prince's Love Symbol on them. Bruce explained that he had removed some decals from the car a while back, but the shape was still visible. We laughed and I asked Mark if he had had a good time at the dance-party. He said that he had and Apollonia Kotero and André Cymone had been there. He also told me that sadly, he had not managed to get to the Electric Fetus to meet Susannah Melvoin.

On the five minute walk up Audubon Road to Paisley Park, we talked about the day we had had and the night he had enjoyed Downtown. I also spoke to Bruce, who told me that he was a tech entrepreneur. As we walked together, he elaborated on this a little and it was clear that he was an astute businessman who was very successful. Bruce told me that he was from Kansas City and he had driven up to Minneapolis for *Celebration 2017*. I mentioned my friend Michael who works as an announcer at KCUR-FM in Kansas City. Bruce smiled and said that he was aware of him.

We reached the complex and headed inside for the final day of events at Prince's home. As we entered the building, Bruce spoke to one of the Paisley Park staffers as if he knew him. It turned out that he did. Bruce told me that he had visited Paisley Park several times since Prince's passing.

We proceeded to the Soundstage and took our seats. As with every other day of *Celebration 2017*, the day's proceedings were to begin with us all sitting in the auditorium to watch a film of Prince performing live in concert.

Joel Weinshanker greeted us and talked about the events over the last few days. He told us that we were now a part of Prince's history, and that *Celebration 2017* would be remembered as the inaugural celebration of Prince's life and work at Paisley Park. He said that we would be offered the first chance to purchase tickets for next year's gathering of Prince *fam*, and thanked us – and the artists and associates of Prince who had taken part – for making *Celebration 2017* such a success. He then handed over to our host Damaris Lewis, who echoed his sentiments, telling us that Prince would be proud of the respect and love his *fam* have shown his home over the course of *Celebration 2017*. She reiterated our importance in carrying Prince's legacy forward for future generations and said she hoped to see us again in 2018. As Damaris left the stage, the lights went down and for the last time on this trip we watched a Prince show on the big screen.

The show – again never officially released – featured a performance recorded in Japan in 1990. The concert – which took place in August of that year at the Tokyo Dome – was part of the so-called *Nude Tour*. This concert tour was a more stripped-back affair – hence the 'Nude' in its title – than previous tours Prince had undertaken, and featured a tight greatest hits set that focused on Prince's desire to attract a more youthful audience. He jettisoned the horn section of his band and introduced the original line-up of the New Power Generation for the first time. In keeping with the idea of a less-extravagant show which was aimed at cutting costs – his previous tours had often been prohibitively expensive – Prince performed on the most basic stage he had played on for years. Concentrating on the recent *Batman* soundtrack album he had released the year before, and the 1990 *Graffiti Bridge* soundtrack album – released just two weeks before the show we were about to watch – the sets were a much leaner affair.

We settled back in our seats as the show opened. Rising up through the stage, Prince – his hair longer and looser than previously seen and sporting almost a full beard – launched into 'The Future' from the *Batman* LP. He was flanked by the male dancers he had incorporated into his live shows at this time. They were known as the 'Game Boyz' and comprised Damon Dickson, Tony M, and Kirk Johnson. Damon and Tony had appeared on the NPG panel on our first day at Paisley Park. Prince danced with Damon and Kirk in a tightly choreographed sequence. Tony M performed rap vocals on the *Nude Tour* and the subsequent album *Diamonds and Pearls* from 1991 as well as its follow up, the unpronounceable album from 1992 known to *fam* as *Love Symbol*.

'The Future' led into '1999' which Prince played poker-straight, opting to stick to the original arrangement. The lead vocal was shared between Prince and singer and keyboardist Rosie Gaines, who was another new addition to the New Power Generation line-up. Several years after leaving Prince's band, Rosie achieved a top five single in the UK with her smash hit 'Closer than Close'.

'1999' morphed into 'Housequake', a hard-hitting rap track from the *Sign o' the Times* album from 1987. Again, the arrangement adhered closely to the original version until just before the song ended, when 'Sexy Dancer' from Prince's self-titled 1979 album appeared for an all-too-brief moment.

One of the biggest hits of Prince's career, 'Kiss' – from the 1986 *Parade* album – followed, and it incorporated elements of Monty Norman's 'James Bond Theme'. The version of 'Purple Rain' that Prince performed next – which included the electrifying guitar solo the song is famous for – was a shortened version than that which appears on the 1984 soundtrack album of the same name, and it was followed by the last number we would see from the film. Prince introduced it with a playful, "Tokyo, I love you baby," before enquiring if the audience loved him. He then asked, "When you go home tonight, would you take me with you?" and the band launched into 'Take Me with U' from *Purple Rain*.

As the song faded out, the lights went up and the audience rose to its feet to applaud. Every clip we had seen during *Celebration 2017* had been incredible, and reinforced the oft-held notion by *fam* and critics alike that Prince was the pre-eminent rock and roll performer of his generation.

Leaving the Soundstage, we quickly made our way to the marquee for food. It was approaching 6.00pm and I hadn't eaten since breakfast twelve hours earlier. Entering the food court, we saw that the centre tables in the room had been filled with cardboard boxes of purple bags. Staffers were manning the tables, and we noticed that the bags were full of official Paisley Park merchandise.

Before we'd set off from the UK, we'd spotted on the official Paisley Park website that there was a limited hardback *Celebration 2017* coffee table book available for purchase that could only be collected at Prince's home in Chanhassen. There was no postage option available, which meant that you could only purchase it if you were attending *Celebration 2017*, or knew someone else who was going. I had quickly ordered a copy. When we'd arrived at Paisley Park on the first day, I'd bought another three beautiful books that, when added to the one I had ordered before I left the UK, formed a set of four. It was the online book that was waiting for me in the marquee on our last day at *Celebration 2017*.

We joined the queue to collect our books, and realising that we were running out of time to get something to eat, we decided to skip dinner at Paisley Park and go out for a late night meal after we left *Celebration 2017* at 10.00pm. We collected our books – the bags had our names printed on them and the staffers only released them when they had been checked against our photo identification passes – and headed to our next event. It was a panel discussion back in the Soundstage.

We grabbed seats close to the stage and the screen displayed the words 'New Power Generation & 3rdeyegirl 2001 – 2016'. A cheer went up as the guest speakers walked onto the stage. Smiling, they took their seats. From left to right, they were *Celebration 2017* host Damaris Lewis, The NPG's Shelby J, Donna Grantis, guitarist with 3rdeyegirl, Adrian Crutchfield of the NPG Hornz, and Kip Blackshire of The NPG.

Damaris – wearing a pair of knee-high purple boots Prince would have undoubtedly loved – acted as the interviewer for this segment, and after introducing the members of the panel to the audience, she asked them to talk about how their involvement with Prince came about.

Shelby J began, and told us the story of how Larry Graham

– bassist in Prince's band – had contacted her, asking her to come to Las Vegas to play a show at Prince's *Per4ming Live 3121* residency at the club he had opened at the Rio Hotel and Casino in November 2006. On a related note – and in an act of spectacularly bad timing on my part – my wife and I stayed ten minutes from the Rio at the Luxor Hotel in Las Vegas mere months before Prince's residency began. Thinking she was there simply to fill in for a sick backing singer for a single performance, Shelby began the rehearsal for that night's show. During the run-through, she heard a voice over the PA repeatedly asking her to sing a certain part again and again. Shelby suddenly found that she was actually in an impromptu audition when – without warning – Prince walked onto the stage from behind and began to sing alongside her, his face just inches from hers. She cracked a joke about worrying if she'd eaten something earlier he might have been able to smell. Shelby was offered a position with the New Power Generation on the spot – which she accepted – and she was told to immediately begin preparing for the half-time show at Super Bowl XLI in Miami. Prince's routine at the game – watched by 75,000 in the stadium and an estimated global audience of 140 million – has consistently been voted the greatest half-time show of all time. Shelby laughed as she told us how excited she was at being told she'd be performing at the show. Her infectious smile warmed the entire Soundstage.

Next we heard from Donna Grantis. I'd met her at the show Shelby J had performed a few days earlier at the Dakota Jazz Club, where she had joined the band onstage for a few numbers. She spoke softly about Prince, and it was clear that she was still deeply affected by his passing. Telling us how she grew up in Ontario and had learned to play guitar as a teenager, Donna laughed as she explained how she had posted clips of her playing on the internet – hoping to be spotted – and one day receiving an email from Prince's management. Damaris Lewis laughed and said, "You never know when your audition's going to come." Prince had asked his drummer Hannah Ford to find a female guitarist, and Hannah had seen Donna's clips online. The email asked her to learn 'Endorphinemachine', 'Let's Go Crazy', and 'She's Always in My Hair' from Prince's catalogue. Donna was then invited to go to Paisley Park. Donna recalled how cold it was in Minneapolis that December. She confessed to us that it had been her desire to work with Prince ahead of any other musician, and said she was thrilled when she got the call to travel to Minneapolis and begin her association with him. Donna told us that she was not sure what the band would be called, but had seen their logo – a girl with three eyes putting her finger to her lips – on flight cases and artwork. Prince only unveiled the name of the band – 3rdeyegirl – as they began rehearsals for the *Live Out Loud Tour*, which was scheduled to begin in April 2013.

Saxophonist Adrian Crutchfield was a member of Prince's band from 2012 to 2015. As leader of the eleven-piece horn section – dubbed the NPG Hornz – that Prince used throughout the latter period of his career, Adrian performed on what were to become Prince's final recordings, *Hitnrun Phase Two* and the as-yet unreleased *Black Is The New Black*. He told us how he grew up in Charlotte, North Carolina and received his first saxophone as a young boy when the musician Kenny G pulled him onto the stage during a concert in Virginia and let him play. Adrian talked of his audition for Prince, and said that his former bandleader was already well aware of Adrian's abilities even before they met. He said that Prince always encouraged him to pursue a career with his own music, and never be content to just be a sideman. When Adrian told Prince that playing with him was enough, he said that Prince became upset and made him promise to fulfil his potential. Adrian promised Prince that he would. Since leaving the NPG, Adrian teaches music at Catawba College in North Carolina, where he has put Prince's music on the syllabus.

"It's my way of keeping his legacy alive," he said.

At one point during the discussion, a member of the audience was addressed by Adrian. He told them, "You are the Next Power

Generation," and he asked us to teach our kids about the man who had brought us all here.

"If we do that," he said, "Prince is immortal."

Leap – Adrian's superb 2017 album – includes the number 'Slow Down', in which he directly addresses his fallen mentor and friend.

Kip Blackshire is a keyboard player and vocalist who was a member of the New Power Generation from 1999 to 2001. He told us how his audition for Prince's band was a particularly awkward moment for him, as Prince asked him to sing 'Little Red Corvette' on stage in the room we were sitting in. Kip – a gospel singer before his tenure with the band – confessed to us that he had never actually heard the song before that moment.

Damaris was taken aback. "You'd never heard 'Little Red Corvette'?" she asked, incredulous.

Kip smiled and said, "Yes. I come from a religious background. We weren't allowed to listen to Prince as kids."

The audience laughed and Kip continued, telling us that he managed to get through the song – lyric sheet in hand – to a level that Prince found acceptable, and he was offered a spot in the band. Kip subsequently performed alongside Prince on the *Hitnrun Tour* from late 2000 to mid-2001, and the short *A Celebration 2001* tour that the band also undertook in June of that year.

The members of the guest panel spoke with great affection – and admiration – about Prince and the influence he'd had on their lives, and as the discussion drew to a conclusion it struck me that it had been a similar story with every other discussion we had seen at Paisley Park over the past four days. Without exception, each associate of this incredible man had shown him or herself to be as much a Prince *fam* as the audience gathered at this inaugural celebration of his life and work. I'd been genuinely moved by the love that they all shared for him – and for us. Their bond with each other as brothers and sisters of an exclusive family was strong, and it was a fine testament to Prince's love of nurturing talent in his fellow artists. With boundless enthusiasm, a staggering work ethic, and never wanting anything in return, he gave of his time – and talent – selflessly. Over the course of his entire career – ultimately spanning five decades – the development of gifted artists he admired or felt he could help had always been an important part of what makes Prince so special to us all. The gratitude of the musicians, designers, and artists we had met at *Celebration 2017* and whom he chose to "Shine his light on" – as The Revolution's Wendy Melvoin had so eloquently put it – unquestionably expresses how they feel about the way he championed their creative abilities, and it touched me to think that he has affected all of our lives, collectively. As an idol, mentor, brother, and guiding force, he is theirs as much as he is ours. As we stood in his house – gathered to celebrate his life – we were as one in our appreciation of this extraordinary little comet.

We had two events left at Paisley Park today. The next one promised to be the biggest insight we would get into the way Prince lived and worked and – if the air of excitement around me was any indicator – it was the element of *Celebration 2017* that many attendees had been looking forward to the most. In a few minutes, we would be given a guided tour of Prince's recording complex in full. Following the sign for Group C – the letter stamped on our photo identification passes – we met our tour guide. She told us that we had to stay together in our group as the time allocated for the walk-through was pretty tight – just thirty-five minutes as there were a lot of people to get through the building – and I breathed a sigh of relief that back in the UK I had also booked us on a more in-depth ninety-minute tour which was scheduled to take place tomorrow after *Celebration 2017* finished, just before we departed from Minneapolis for good. I'd felt that a final trip through Prince's house would be a fitting end to our time in his hometown.

Our group gathered at the doorway to Paisley Park and we were ready to enter this incredible complex to commemorate the work of a man who has united us through a mutual love of his artistry.

The idea for Paisley Park was borne of Prince's desire to build a creative space in which to work and play. The complex was the germination of a seed that had been planted in Prince's mind long before the first construction drawing was made. In the early '80s, an alternative scene had emerged from Los Angeles which had been dubbed the 'Paisley Underground' after the clothing West Coast rock bands of the '70s had worn. The preferred fashion featured a twisted droplet or teardrop motif and this burgeoning movement of creative artisans featured an aesthetic that combined elements of both post-punk and folk. Prince – the fledgling rock god who was emerging in his own right as an important figure in popular music at this time – embraced this counterculture wholeheartedly, and subsequently began incorporating paisley prints into his outfits. The rehearsal and recording facility he had purchased on Flying Cloud Drive – which we had visited earlier – had already been christened 'Paisley Park'. In 1985 – having fully absorbed the influences the movement had built its foundation on – Prince released the *Around the World in a Day* album. Included in this set was a psychedelic single – also called 'Paisley Park' – and the song's lyrics spoke of a magical utopia where 'colourful people' were not inhibited by the limits or expectations imposed by the physical world. The concept of 'Paisley Park' was the genesis of what would become Prince's home and workplace in Minneapolis. The provision of an artistic hub for the local community to utilise was an important factor too. Prince's canny business acumen ensured that it was one that paid off. Upon its public opening in 1987, the smart new facility held three days of special events, and Paisley Park quickly became a bustling hive of activity.

Plans for the construction of Paisley Park were first drawn up in 1985, and the work was undertaken by Metropolitan Mechanical Contractors, Inc, a local firm from Eden Prairie. Previously, the company had been responsible for the construction of Mall of America in Bloomington, which is ten miles south of Downtown

Minneapolis. It is the largest shopping mall in the United States in terms of store number and total floor area.

Designed by a young architect named Bret Thoeny of BOTO Design, the 65,000 square foot building Prince commissioned was amongst the first ever requested by a musician to house an entire industry under one roof. Taking two years to complete, the building – which is estimated to have cost ten million dollars to construct – gave Prince the freedom to create at will.

Before Paisley Park, musicians had simply used a number of locations for different elements of their work. This proved to be time consuming and expensive. Travelling to recording and photography studios often meant flying to other parts of the country. Rehearsing for tours and performances frequently involved hiring venues large enough to accommodate huge amounts of equipment and people. More often than not these would be out of town. This would facilitate more travel, which again could drive up costs. Socialising would usually be done at home, or in clubs where artists would be unable to relax due to fans and the press providing a constant distraction. Prince changed all of that, creating a playground and business complex which enabled him to do all of those things in the same building.

Many elements of Paisley Park's design came from Prince himself. His fascination with Egypt led to the roof skylights being constructed in the form of glass pyramids, and his insistence on having a world-class rehearsal and performance space was of utmost importance. Prince wanted a stage with enough room for stadium-sized show run-throughs. By creating this facility, he could keep increasingly ambitious set designs, new musical arrangements, and dance routines under wraps until he was ready to reveal them to adoring *fam* at his incredible sold-out shows around the world. Prince envisaged that the Soundstage would also be used by television and film crews and had production offices, fully-appointed dressing rooms, and even a scenery repair workshop built, as well as a fully-staffed wardrobe department. A team of skilled craftsmen and women would design and manufacture his and his band member's otherworldly clothes. Everything Prince needed was kept in-house.

Perhaps the most important element of Paisley Park though – for Prince at least – were the state-of-the-art recording studios he installed. Virtually all of his studio albums from *The Black Album* in 1987 through to *Hitnrun Phase Two* – released physically just three months before his passing in April 2016 – were recorded there. Studio A is a fifteen hundred-square-foot studio featuring an acoustically live room with granite walls. The facility has a wooden isolation room and a vocal booth that has two isolation rooms and a control room. Boasting a Solid State Logic eighty channel console, the studio is digital and analogue ready. 1988's spiritual *Lovesexy* album and *Diamonds and Pearls* from 1991 were committed to tape in this room. Studio B is slightly smaller at a thousand square-feet and is broken down into one live room, one vocal room and a central room. Featuring a forty-eight track console, this studio is built totally to Prince's specifications. *Sign o' the Times* – Prince's tour de force from 1987 – was recorded right here. A third recording studio also exists at Paisley Park. Known as Studio C, it is slightly smaller than Studio B. Originally a rehearsal room, it features a thirty-two track mixing desk.

We headed through the lobby and into the Atrium. It smelled of flowers. The whole building did. The doors leading off this area that were previously closed to us were now open. Some of them contained outfits and instruments. We assembled in the centre of the Atrium between two purple velour couches, and our guide pointed out features of the space. On the west side of the Atrium on the balcony above us was a huge ornate birdcage. Prince's doves Divinity and Majesty live there. Also on the west side of the Atrium was the 'Little Kitchen'. Part-glazed wooden doors ran the length of the room. I wandered over to take a look inside. It looked like an ordinary kitchen in any home. At one end, there were two diner-style booths. The kitchen was fitted out with all the appliances you would expect to find in a modern food preparation area. Prince's espresso machine was there, and his microwave too. At the right end of the kitchen, a small living room had been created. There was a couch with a little table in front of it facing a television. The table had magazines casually strewn across it. Prince apparently enjoyed watching sports in this room, while fixing snacks for his guests. It warmed me to know that – despite owning an incredible home that most of us can only dream about – he lived like a normal person, eating his meals in front of the TV in this charming little room. I smiled when I saw the couch. I have a couch in my kitchen. We never use it. The tour guide told us that the 'Little Kitchen' was Prince's favourite place to hang out at Paisley Park.

Above the doors to the kitchen – and directly above my head – was a small frosted acrylic case which was mounted high on the wall, overlooking the Atrium. The case housed a miniature replica of Paisley Park. On the front of the scale reproduction was a large bejewelled Love Symbol. It was his beloved purple. I caught my breath as I looked at it for the first time on my journey. This was the final resting place of Prince Rogers Nelson.

As I stood beneath him, my heart ached and I felt an immense sadness that he was no longer here. Around me, I could hear people weeping softly. And then I started to cry too. I stayed there – alone – for just a minute or two. This was the first time since his passing a year ago that it had felt real to me. I'd known all along that he was here, of course. I'd walked past him every time we had come into his home. But I'd avoided looking at his urn. I'm not sure why I did it. I don't really have an answer. Looking back now, a few months later, I think, perhaps, that I may have thought that if I didn't acknowledge the fact that he was no longer around, he might simply just walk in the door. Funny that, isn't it? I had clearly been in denial. As I stood in front of my idol in the Atrium of this incredible place where he will live forever, it was only now that I realised that I had pushed the thought of him dying out of my mind completely while I'd been here. But now I was faced with the truth. And it hurt so much. In what I expect will turn out to be one of the saddest occasions of my life, I paid my respects to the man who helped shape my formative years.

Eventually, Jonathan came over to me.

"Are you okay?" he asked.

"I will be, I guess," I replied.

As I walked away from Prince, I realised that I would be here again tomorrow. It would be the last time I'd ever see him.

"See you soon," I said.

Wiping my eyes, I rejoined the group and we began to explore the rooms around the Atrium.

At the opposite end of the Atrium from the kitchen were four rooms. The door to each was a different colour and depicts an image of Prince from four different eras of his career. From the left they were *Dirty Mind*, *Controversy*, *Diamonds and Pearls*, and finally, *Sign o' the Times*. Behind the purple couch nearest the *Sign o' the Times* Room – and facing the entrance to the Atrium – was the *Lovesexy* Room.

Dedicated to the 1980 album, the *Dirty Mind* Room contained an early notebook of Prince's that has the lyrics to 'Soft and Wet', his first single, written in it. It was dated '77 and signed with a heart over the 'i' in his name.

The *Controversy* Room – named after the 1981 album – contained Prince's Mad Cat guitar, which we had seen earlier in the week when we had first arrived at Paisley Park.

The *Diamonds and Pearls* Room featured outfits relating to the 1991 album. Prince's incredible yellow suit with dozens of purple buttons was there. His pearl-covered jacket was in this room too. As I looked at them, 'Gett Off' – the lead single from *Diamonds and Pearls* – was playing.

Stepping into the *Sign o' the Times* Room, my heart leapt. A video screen played the concert movie of the same name. In front of me was the peach drum-kit used in the movie. Next to it was the peach Cloud guitar Prince played in 1987. Both of these items are visible on the front sleeve of the *Sign o' the Times* album. Standing next to the drum-kit was Prince's patchwork denim jacket. The work that had gone into this intricate coat was amazing. I'd seen it in the movie thirty years ago, but the level of detail was lost on the big screen. It's genuinely a work of art. Alongside the jacket was Prince's white faux-fur coat. It was the one he wore in the 'U Got the Look' promo video. The Cloud guitar featured in the video too.

Crossing over to the other side of the Atrium, I entered the *Lovesexy* Room. In it were outfits and instruments from what I – and many other Prince *fam* – consider to be his greatest tour, which took place in 1988. The long mint-green and black asymmetrical jacket – with *Lovesexy* down one arm and odd-sized buttons – that I'd seen him wear almost three decades ago, was there. Next to it was Prince's green cropped jacket with metal pendants hanging from it. It is covered in letters and numbers. A stunning black brocade suit embroidered with turquoise flowers was on display nearby. It was complemented by Prince's matching shoes. In front of the outfits was the original 'Model C' guitar that he used around this time. Its outlandish jagged design is still utterly outrageous thirty years after its construction. The *Lovesexy* album sleeve and the words '👁 Wish U Heaven' covered a wall each, and the others were festooned with photos of the New Power Generation who played on this tour. Each member of the band had a quote written on the wall.

To the left of the *Sign o' the Times* Room as I left it – and a little further down the corridor – was Prince's personal office. Stepping inside it was a surreal moment. This was where he conducted his business affairs. There were desks at either end of the large room and behind each of them were floor-to-ceiling bookcases crammed with tomes on the Arts and History. Encyclopaedias and books on poetry jostled for space alongside travel journals, and piles of papers sat in in-trays on the beautifully designed tables. Prince's desk was smaller than standard and was perfectly proportioned for him. I spotted a Bible, reference books on Egypt, and a book entitled *In Praise of Black Women: Ancient African Queens*. The room had everything you would expect to find in any well-appointed office, but it was unmistakeably different to any other workspace I've ever been in. It had a gold floor for a start. On the far wall was a stereo system with a turntable. On Prince's desk was a pile of LP records. I spotted a copy of the classic

Cookin' with the Miles Davis Quintet from 1957. The decor was incredibly opulent and gorgeous original works of art adorned the walls. Underneath the window was a small table covered in framed photos of what looked to be Prince's family and close friends. One was of Prince's parents, Mattie and John L Nelson, who have both now sadly passed. A lump caught in my throat when I spotted it. Crossing to the other side of the room, we left the office using the opposite door to the one we entered – there were two – and stepped back into the corridor. Opposite the office door was a tiny recess with a mural of greenery and undergrowth inside it. The alcove had a telephone and a small desk in it.

We walked single file through a long narrow hallway in the corner of the Atrium to the right of the 'Little Kitchen'. We approached the studios and stopped for a moment to look at a beautiful mural on the wall, opposite the door to Studio A. Created by Sam Jennings in 2007, the 'Influence Wall' is a highly-stylised mural that depicts the musical heroes that played a part in shaping Prince's music and style over the course of his career. It also shows the band members and musicians that Prince has in turn influenced. Prince – in a photo that was originally planned as the cover for his 2009 album *Lotusflow3r* – is in the centre of the mural, his arms outstretched. To his left, Stevie Wonder, Sly Stone, George Clinton, and a plethora of classic artists are depicted. For keen music fans it is possible to make myriad connections to Prince's work from theirs. To his right, members of all of his bands are shown alongside artists who have cited him as a significant influence on their careers. For a minute, we played 'Name the musician', and successfully managed to identify all of them.

As we entered Studio A, our guide told us some of the artists that have recorded here. Madonna, REM and Celine Dion were the names I caught. I wasn't really paying much attention. As I looked around me at the other people breathing in this rarefied air, it appeared that nobody was. We were all taking in the experience in our own ways. I walked up to the dark glass of the control room and peered through to the console beyond. I could see Prince's famous Linn LM-1 drum machine standing next to it. There was also a vintage synthesiser. The reporter from Radio New Zealand – who I'd spoken to two days earlier at the candlelit vigil at the Riley Creek underpass – was standing next to me. Her eyes were closed. She was crying quietly and as I looked at her I saw that she was visibly shaking. I thought about all the times I had bought a new Prince album throughout my life and the excitement and anticipation they had brought me, and it felt surreal to be standing in the very room where they were created. I imagined Prince at work here – as he recorded the hundreds of songs I love so much – and I wondered which parts of the studio he had used for each.

The studio was beautifully constructed. There were tactile surfaces all around me. I couldn't resist the urge to run my hands up the carpet-lined walls and along the edges of the isolation booths. I noticed that others were doing it too. It felt important to leave some of my DNA in this room. As we looked around, I was suddenly aware that there was soft music playing quietly in the background. Our tour guide told us that it was an unreleased instrumental track by Prince. I walked to a corner of the room that is unoccupied in an effort to hear it more clearly but I didn't manage to take it in much, as we were then shepherded out of Studio A – another party had just entered – and we were taken into the smaller Studio C.

As we filed into Studio C – Studio B was not included on this tour and is only accessible as part of the VIP Paisley Park package – I was surprised by how small it was. By the time we had all entered the room – there were around thirty of us in total – it was pretty full. Looking around, I could see that – like the previous room – the recording facility was finished to an almost impossible standard. The fittings and surfaces were of an impeccable quality, and I touched every surface, again hoping that a small part of me would rub off in the amazing space Prince had created. As I did this, I was reminded of the time I did the same thing inside the Graceland mansion in

Memphis. Sorry *again*, Joel. While I'm not a musician and I have no experience of working in a studio environment, recording equipment has always fascinated me. I stared at the beautifully complex consoles – they were to me, anyway – imagining talented engineers and technicians as well as Prince himself working at them to produce famous albums that have sold in their millions around the world. As we left Studio C, we headed to the next area. Known as the *Purple Rain* Room – the movie was playing on a huge screen at one end – it wasn't hard to see why this moniker had been chosen.

The walls of the *Purple Rain* Room were adorned with murals from the period. The room was bathed in purple light, and I was drawn to the centre of the space. Standing there – right before my eyes – was Prince's iconic motorcycle from the 1984 movie. I walked across to it. The bike was inside a small enclosure – thirty feet long by fifteen feet wide – in the middle of the room.

In *Purple Rain*, Prince rides a customised 1981 Honda CM400. It is finished – of course – in his trademark purple and features a 1970's Craig Vetter Windjammer fairing and a passenger seat with pink velour inserts and a sissy bar. The Honda features prominently in promotional posters for the movie, and on the sleeve of the *Purple Rain* album itself. And it was right there. I've had a picture of this actual bike in every home I've lived in since I was thirteen years old.

With it were several artefacts from the movie. As I walked around the perimeter of the enclosure, I looked at the objects on display. There was the outfit that Prince wore at the climax of the film when he walked onstage at First Avenue and performed the title number from *Purple Rain*. The long purple trench coat and white ruffled shirt were three feet in front of me. I suddenly realised something. It wasn't the right trench coat. I pointed it out to Jonathan. The one we were looking at was the lamé one Prince wore in the '1999' and 'Little Red Corvette' promotional videos from 1982. It was shimmery, whereas the *Purple Rain* coat was satin and solid purple. Laughing at this error, I stood and looked at the outfit for a while. It was incredibly small. I knew Prince was a diminutive guy – I've seen him up close a lot of times – but looking at his clothes, it sank in just how petite he was.

Next to the *Purple Rain* coat that wasn't, there was another outfit. This one was a multi-coloured suit from the *1999 Tour*. Complete with the ruched trousers and incredible high-heeled ankle boots he wore at this time, the outfit is utterly decadent. Nobody but Prince could wear something so outrageous, I thought to myself. I joked to Mark that I'd struggle to get the waist over my thigh. And I'm not even a big guy.

The next incredible artefact was recognisable to anyone who has seen *Purple Rain* or Prince in concert in the '80s. It was his famous white Cloud guitar. The actual guitar he had played in the movie. It was built in 1983 by Dave Rusan, the luthier I'd seen in the guitar discussion on Friday just before we'd watched The Revolution play. I longed to touch it, and I probably could have if I'd leaned across a little. It was no more than three or four feet from me. It was the same with the other artefacts, by the way. Many of them were not in cases. Respectfully though, nobody even thought of doing it. The white Cloud is still the most beautiful guitar I've ever seen.

Moving along, the next thing I saw blew my mind again. It was Prince's Academy Award. Within touching distance was the Oscar statuette he won for Best Original Song Score at the 1984 Academy Awards. He was the last artist to ever receive this award.

The *Purple Rain* soundtrack is the album most people associate with Prince. Featuring the smash hits 'When Doves Cry', 'Let's Go Crazy', 'Purple Rain', 'I Would Die 4 U', and 'Take Me With U', the record – which captured the zeitgeist perfectly – finally established Prince as a cultural icon, catapulting him to global superstardom. *Purple Rain* has sold over twenty million copies worldwide, and is widely regarded by critics as one of the greatest albums in history. It regularly tops polls as the greatest soundtrack album ever made, and it currently stands as the third-biggest selling soundtrack LP of all time. In 2012, *Purple Rain* was added to the Library of Congress' National Recording Registry. The registry is a list of sound recordings that are deemed 'Culturally, historically, or aesthetically important'. When the dust settles on the history of twentieth century popular music, *Purple Rain* will most likely be the record Prince will be remembered for.

Next to Prince's Academy Award was a slightly dog-eared leather-bound notebook. It was the obligatory purple and was stencilled in gold with the words *Purple Rain*, and in the bottom right corner, *Prince*. This was Prince's personal diary which contains notes and ideas he would jot down for the movie, before and during its production. To Prince *fam*, it's a priceless artefact and a genuine piece of history. Known to be an incredibly prolific talent with a seemingly endless supply of energy, Prince was a constant ball of creativity, and I longed to see inside the notebook to see what ideas he had come up with and whether any of them had made the finished movie.

I walked around the other side of the small enclosure as the tour guide told us that this room was once used as a basketball court, which made me smile. The last item I came to was incredible. It was Prince's Yamaha CP80 electric piano from the *Purple Rain* movie. As I looked at it, I pictured the scene from the film where Prince performs 'The Beautiful Ones' – one of my favourite songs and one of my favourite scenes – while sitting at this very instrument. Again it is a shade of lilac – most *Purple Rain* related items are – and I could see that the top of the piano was battered and worn. Scrapes, scratches and cuts cover its surface.

"They're caused by Prince's boot heels when he used to jump off the piano onstage," the tour guide told us.

The piano was the one Prince used throughout the *Purple Rain Tour*. Seeing the personal effects of my musical hero had left me with memories that I will treasure. With a heavy heart I left the *Purple Rain* Room and headed to the next part of the tour.

Graffiti Bridge is a Prince-directed feature-length 1990 movie which was shot almost entirely inside Paisley Park's Soundstage. His final film, it is the spiritual follow-up to *Purple Rain*, and again features Prince as 'The Kid' battling his arch-enemy Morris Day. This time, they are each trying to gain total control over a nightclub that has been bequeathed to them both by Billy, the fictional owner of First Avenue in *Purple Rain*. The area we now entered was known as the *Graffiti Bridge/Under the Cherry Moon* Room.

Like the room before it, the first thing I saw was a motorcycle. Again it was a Honda CM400, but the paintjob had been modified – from purple to black – and the chrome fittings were now gold-plated. Behind the bike was Prince's tasselled black leather jacket from the movie. It featured an enormous metal Love Symbol on the back. Above the door to the *Graffiti Bridge/Under the Cherry Moon* Room, the huge neon 'Glam Slam' symbol – which was originally over the entrance to the club of the same name we'd visited in Downtown Minneapolis – lit the exit.

Next to the *Graffiti Bridge* motorcycle were some of the props from the 1986 *Under the Cherry Moon* movie. The white suit Prince was wearing in the scene from the movie in which his character – Christopher Tracy – danced with the film's female protagonist, Mary Sharon, was truly beautiful. Immaculately tailored with wide shoulders and a tapered waist that was impossibly small, it featured an exquisite monochrome paisley motif and to me it looked as sharp now as it did in 1986. It's one of my favourite Prince outfits from any era and I was thrilled to see it up close. Again, I marvelled at how small it was. A large screen on the wall just behind the suit showed a clip of the dance scene. Next to the screen was a framed vintage movie poster for *Under the Cherry Moon*. The floor in this part of the room had a black and white checkerboard design.

Next to the suit – below the video screen – were some custom guitar amplifiers that were covered in the same patterned material, and a drum-kit, which was similarly decorated. These were used on the *Parade Tour* from 1986. This was The Revolution's final tour with Prince, and he dissolved the band a month after it ended.

We emerged from the *Graffiti Bridge/Under the Cherry Moon* Room and found ourselves in another hallway. This one was known as the 'Awards Corridor'. At chest height on either side of us, small rectangular recesses – perhaps twelve inches high – were cut into the walls at regular intervals. These little recesses contained Prince's numerous awards. They were all there. Grammy Awards, MTV Music Awards, American Music Awards, Golden Globes, and of course our very own Brit Awards from back in the UK. As I looked at them, I remembered that as a young boy I'd watched him receive these ones on television. I recalled everyone talking about Prince at school the following day. How enigmatic he was. How outrageously he was dressed. And I remembered some of my friends – who knew I was besotted with him – congratulating me on the success of my musical hero, almost as if I was in some way responsible for him winning. Passing through this corridor inside Paisley Park, I was proud to see that there appeared to be more Brits than any other trophy. At the end of the corridor we came across the *Black Album* Room. Tantalisingly, the door was locked and a tiny sign on it said, "No Entry". I smiled at this and wondered if it was a wry practical joke on Prince's part, referring to the infamous album he shelved at the last minute in 1987.

All too soon, the guided tour was over. I was already looking forward to the expanded version we had booked for tomorrow. We headed back to the Soundstage in preparation for the final event of *Celebration 2017*. It was a concert that incorporated two of Prince's bands.

Entering the auditorium I could see that the concert had already started. It was strange to see members of 3rdeyegirl and the New Power Generation perform together, and I wondered if *Celebration 2017* was the first time they had combined their formidable talents in front of an audience.

Featuring Kip Blackshire, Shelby J, Liv Warfield, and Tony M on vocals, Donna Grantis and Levi Seacer, Jr on guitar, Ida Nielsen and Dywane Thomas, Jr – aka Mono Neon – on bass, Prince's former bandleader Morris Hayes and Tommy Barbarella on keyboards, Kirk Johnson on drums, and several members of the NPG Hornz, the combined forces of two of Prince's bands created a thrilling noise. Things took a surreal turn when they were joined for several numbers by none other than Prince's childhood friend and member of his very first backing band, André Cymone. André looked razor sharp in a killer grey suit and a dapper Stacy Adams-type hat with a feather tucked into the band. He performed songs from early in Prince's career including 'Uptown' – from the 1980 *Dirty Mind* album – and 'Do, Me Baby', from 1981's *Controversy* LP.

The remainder of the show was a superb greatest hits selection covering the '80s and '90s. I noticed that there were no 3rdeyegirl numbers in the set. I could only assume that the extended band line-up may not have had time to learn them fully. The band tore through classics from the height of the NPG era and as 'Cream' and 'Diamonds and Pearls' echoed around the Soundstage, the audience was dancing and clapping for all its worth. Tony M displayed formidable rapping skills and, for several numbers, including 'Kiss' and 'U Got the Look', lead vocals were performed by Shelby J and Liv Warfield.

As I watched the show, I noticed that the two women dancing next to me were enjoying the concert very much and were swaying in time with the music. One was Kim Berry – Prince's hairstylist for almost three decades – and the other was Debbie McGuan. Debbie was Prince's long-time designer. I'd seen them both yesterday on the fashion discussion panel in the NPG Music Club. I smiled at them and said, "Hello," and they smiled and said, "Hi" back. I turned my attention back to the music, and smiled to myself. As I did so, Prince's half-brother Alfred walked right past me toward the back of the Soundstage. He was accompanied by a woman. He smiled as he went past. I was amazed that he was just casually walking around Paisley Park amongst the crowd. Alfred passed by Mark too – who was about twenty feet behind me – and I motioned to him but he didn't see me or Alfred as he was too busy dancing to the music.

More songs followed. 1985's 'Pop Life' led into 'Housequake' from *Sign o' the Times*. As the first chords of 'Purple Rain' began, Shelby and Liv handled vocal duties until suddenly, a film of

Prince – performing the track on the 2011 *Welcome 2 America Tour* – flickered to life on the huge screen onstage. Wearing a shimmering gold shirt and matching pants – and with his hair cut short – he looked phenomenal. As Prince sang his signature number, the band – playing on stage – accompanied him, and it was a genuinely profound moment. People all around the Soundstage were tearful and as I looked around lots of attendees were hugging each other as they watched him. It was incredibly poignant. The clip was a reminder – as if one was needed – that Prince was – and always will be – one of the greatest live performers on the planet.

I looked at Kim Berry, and she wiped her eyes with a tissue and smiled as she looked up at the screen. Debbie was emotional too and I marvelled again at how he had touched all of our lives. As I did so, I wiped my eyes. As with every event I had seen over the past four days at *Celebration 2017*, the show came to an end far too soon.

Ben walked over from where he had been standing.

"That was incredible," he said, smiling broadly. "We might not be able to meet Ida Nielsen at the record store tomorrow," he continued, referring to the fact that we were due to fly at the same time she'd be in-store at the Electric Fetus, "but at least I got to see her onstage at Paisley Park."

We laughed and took our seats for the closing of *Celebration 2017*.

Damaris Lewis addressed us from the stage for the final time. She talked for a few minutes, telling us how much Prince would have enjoyed the past four days and she reiterated the importance of carrying Prince's legacy forward for future generations.

"Tell others what you have seen here. Talk about Prince as much as you can," she asked the audience.

The audience clapped and some people whooped and hollered.

Damaris continued, "He welcomed people here, and it would have warmed his heart to see us all share this incredible experience together." She ended by thanking us for the respect we had shown Paisley Park. "This was Prince's home," she said. "Take care of where *you* call home."

The audience rose to its feet and applauded Prince, Paisley Park and everyone who had made this incredible anniversary week such a success. As I watched, I realised that the atmosphere around the occasion of Prince's passing had been predominantly one of joy rather than solemnity. I felt sure he would have liked that.

The Soundstage lights came up and *Celebration 2017* was over. It had been without doubt one of the greatest weeks of my life. I told Jonathan I'd write down what had happened when we got home, as I was sure to forget all the things we had seen. He agreed that it was a good idea. Although I was saddened that my adventure had almost finished, I was looking forward to getting home and seeing my family. I was just another couple of days away from normality. After the crazy week we had just had, normality was exactly what I needed. Sleep too. But the trip wasn't quite over just yet. We still had another tour of Paisley Park in the morning before we flew home.

Leaving the building took a few minutes as the crowd was moving very slowly. Eventually reaching the line of Paisley Park staffers, we unlocked our phones and stepped outside into the warm Chanhassen night. It was a beautiful evening, and the parking lot was full of people who just wanted to hang out. It seemed no one else wanted *Celebration 2017* to end tonight either. We took some photos of each other standing at the small wooden sign outside the gates of Paisley Park, and Mark and I hugged before he left for Downtown. It had been an absolute pleasure to share my trip with him, and I hoped that he felt the same. I looked at my watch and it was after 10.00pm. We agreed to go back to Buffalo Wild Wings for food – which pleased our resident wings connoisseur Ben – and we walked away from Paisley Park up the eerily silent Audubon Road back to the car.

The drive back to the restaurant was only a few minutes – five at most – and we headed inside. A young guy brought us drinks and I looked around. Locals were out enjoying their Sunday night and I wondered how many – if any – were Prince *fam* and if they were aware of what had been going on this week in their little town. I ordered a chicken salad, and Jonathan and Ben ordered a sharing platter each. As we ate, we looked back over our week in Prince's town. It had been astonishing, and we were all in agreement that as life experiences go, it was going to take some beating. Then they did something that touched me deeply. They thanked me for bringing them. I cleared my throat and laughed, and I told them that it had been my pleasure to do this with them both. And it genuinely had.

We drove back to our hotel on West 78th Street. It was now around midnight and the streets were quiet. As I parked the car, I saw a woman walking into the lobby. I couldn't be sure, but I thought it was someone I recognised. We walked across the parking lot and into the hotel.

People were milling around inside and there was a bit of a commotion. Almost immediately, I spotted Monica, Shelby J's manager. Then I spotted Shelby. And then I saw Liv Warfield from the New Power Generation. She was talking to a lady with red hair. It was none other than Ida Nielsen from 3rdeyegirl.

Shelby was sitting at a desk and a photographer was snapping away in front of her.

Monica said, "Hi," and Shelby waved to us.

Ben was beside himself as Ida – the bassist who he most admires in the world – stood nearby.

"I don't believe this," he said smiling.

"I know," I said, "who needs to go to the record store? Ida has come to us!"

There were no more than fifteen people there in total, and as I looked around I couldn't believe the crazy opportunities this amazing trip had repeatedly afforded us. I grabbed a few snaps of the ladies from Prince's bands and as I talked to Monica and Shelby, I could see Ben was in conversation with Ida. The look on his face was one of pure joy. All of Prince's associates were gracious and thanked us for coming, and we posed for a group photo before bidding them goodnight and returning to our rooms.

That photo is one of hundreds I'd taken there that I'll always treasure. To get this close to people Prince loved and worked with – and to get to know them, even just a tiny bit – had been revelatory. I've known Prince the superstar for as long as I could remember, but this week – and the amazing people we had met and incredible places we had been – had made me feel like I now knew Prince the man. At the beginning of this adventure – when I'd first arrived in the hotel in Chanhassen – my friend Michael in Kansas City had told me that "Minnesota is good country." He hadn't been wrong.

I called my wife. She told me that she and the kids were looking forward to me coming home. We talked for a while and she asked me if the trip had been everything I'd wanted it to be and whether I'd gotten out of it what I had hoped for. I said it had exceeded my expectations enormously. I spoke to the kids, who were getting ready for school.

"I'll see you very soon," I said. Ending the call, I sent my wife the pictures I had taken and emptied my phone.

I decided to pack, figuring it would save time in the morning. Trying to close my suitcase was proving difficult though. I'd bought quite a few things while I had been there: half a dozen books, some prints, a tambourine, and several posters in cardboard tubes. Some of the items were quite cumbersome. There was nothing for it. I'd have to leave some stuff behind. Taking my clothes out of the case, I lay them on the sofa and went through them, electing to leave a couple of sweaters, three pairs of jeans, and a pair of boots. I placed them next to the bed and finished packing. I managed to fit everything in and I lay on the bed, quickly drifting off to sleep after struggling to read the same page of a book five times.

MONDAY

We were due to be at Paisley Park at 10.30am for our final visit. The tour was due to last ninety minutes and our flight was not until 4.10pm. That meant a leisurely final day, which was perfect after all the excitement we'd had over the past week. Meeting in the breakfast area at 8.00am, we loaded our cases into the car and sat down for our last meal at the Country Inn and Suites in Chanhassen. Outside, the sun was shining brightly. Other than the first day we had been here, the weather had been perfect. Although I was excited at the prospect of seeing my family, I was going to miss the city of Minneapolis enormously.

We sat around chatting until 10.00am, and walked outside into the beautiful morning air. Driving up Audubon Road, we arrived back on Park Road and I left the car in our usual spot behind Paisley Park. Ambling up to Prince's home there was an air of stillness over the place. It was the first time we'd seen the complex without lots of people around. The parking lot was almost empty.

We walked to the security gate and I took the tour confirmation print-out from my pocket to hand to the official. As I did so, I looked at it. Our tour was due to start at 9.00am, not 10.30am. I'd got the time wrong, and we were almost ninety minutes late. Our tour party was scheduled to actually leave Paisley Park in ten minutes. I explained to the security officer what had happened and he handed back our confirmation, telling us .to go to the reception area inside the lobby of Paisley Park. We got to the entrance and saw that there was a tour party about to go inside. I spoke to a staffer on the door who pointed us towards the desk. Explaining to the lady there that I had gotten the time wrong for our tour, I asked if we could join the group who were standing around me waiting to commence their visit. She checked our print out and said it would be fine. We bought some purple Paisley Park-branded USB flash drives and joined the group.

Our guide – a good-looking guy named Mitch McGuire – began the tour in the lobby and showed us the lyric that floated along the wall at the foot of the stairs. It was from a track called 'U Make My Sun Shine' from Prince's 2004 album, *The Chocolate Invasion*. We walked into the Atrium, passing beneath the image of Prince's eyes which gazed down at us as we entered his home. I was aware that there were people in this tour party who had not been here before, but I knew what was coming. Mitch stood in the centre of the Atrium with us gathered around him, and he pointed out everything of interest that we could see, including Divinity and Majesty in their beautiful cage high up on the next floor. Mitch said that after Prince's passing, they went silent for a while. I didn't hear what else he said, for as he talked, I walked over to Prince's urn and stood quietly beneath it for a few minutes. To some, it might seem a little too 'showbiz' for his remains to be in full view of everyone that came into the building, but Prince felt most at home in front of an audience so it kind of made sense for him to be here. I felt comforted by that, and also by just being here with him. For me – and the others here – he was the ultimate showman, and for as long as people come to this place he will always be on stage. The atmosphere in the Atrium is deeply respectful and – when it's not full of people – it is a really beautiful place that has a peaceful, calming ambience. The sunshine flooded through the pyramids above our heads, and I was thankful to be there in this serene space. As I stood next to Prince, I was pretty sure that this would be the last time I would ever see him. This thought made me sad, but I was actually happy too. I know that I am lucky to have had this opportunity to say goodbye to him so personally. Not many people are able to visit their idol's home or stand alone at their urn. As I write this now, it is almost four months since I stood on that spot in the Atrium inside Paisley Park, but if I close my eyes I'm right back there. I think I've done that every day since I left.

We headed to the studios. Inside Studio A, Mitch pointed out Prince's Oberheim OB-X synthesizer and his Linn LM-1 drum machine in the control room. The LM-1 is an instrument synonymous with Prince's sound on *1999* and *Purple Rain*. I noticed a solitary microphone hanging down over the huge 80 channel mixing desk, and Mitch told us that instead of the traditional mic in the studio arrangement, this was where Prince actually recorded all of his vocals. He sat down at the desk in the control room – while he was mixing and producing – to record his voice. This information drew gasps from us all. In the isolation booth in the corner, Mitch pointed out Wendy's original purple Rickenbacker guitar. A music stand in Studio A had Prince's handwritten lyrics on it. They are believed to be the words to an unreleased song named 'Stay Cool'. Also on the stand were typed lyrics to 'Look at Me, Look at U' from Prince's final studio album *Hitnrun Phase Two*. I caught my breath. This was all too much. Mitch had given us a lot more information than the first time we'd been in the studio. We were behind the magician's curtain now.

In the *Purple Rain* Room, I was pleased to see that the correct trench coat was now in place and I smiled when I saw it. Returning to the *Graffiti Bridge/Under the Cherry Moon* Room again, we stopped to watch the clip from the movie and Mitch asked if anyone could name the actress who played the French heiress, Mary Sharon. Jonathan and I answered simultaneously that it was the English actress Kristen Scott-Thomas making her feature film debut. Heading toward the Piano Room, we stopped at some guitars that were on display just outside it.

The first was a custom-made psychedelic-hued red and yellow VOX guitar that Prince played throughout the 3rdeyegirl period of his career. I recognised it as the guitar I'd last seen Prince with in Leeds in the UK back in 2014. Next to it was the famous 'Love

Symbol' guitar that Prince used in the '90s. Built by the German luthier Jerry Auerswald, it features heart-shaped tuning pegs. It is finished in gold and is as dramatic a guitar as you will ever see. As I looked at it, I was amazed it had lasted so well, as the parts that jut out of the body at right angles to create the symbol element of the design looked extremely fragile. Jerry is also responsible for creating the 'Model C' guitar that was in the *Lovesexy* Room. The final guitar outside the Piano Room was the last one Prince ever received. Built by British luthier Simon 'Gus' Farmer in East Sussex, the guitar was stunning. It was made from carbon fibre and cedar, and was coloured a rich purple with an abundance of gold plating. It was an astonishing looking instrument and Prince had showed it off just before his passing, having only received it in March 2016.

Entering the Piano Room, the centrepiece, Prince's incredible Schimmel Pegasus grand piano – which had astounded me the first day I had been at Paisley Park – did its job again to the party members who hadn't seen it before. I chuckled as the guy next to me whistled at it. Mitch told us to look out of the window to the left of the yellow couch next to the piano, and there in the loading dock outside was Prince's enormous tour bus. Turning back toward the right side of the room, the doors to the Soundstage were closed. On the wall to the left of the doors was the original artwork for 2001's *The Rainbow Children* album. The painting is called *Reine Keis Quintet*, and it is by St Louis-based artist Cbabi Bayoc. On my first day at Paisley Park, I'd sat next to a larger copy of the artwork hanging in the NPG Music Club, next door to the Soundstage we were about to enter for the final time.

Walking into the Soundstage now that the seats had been removed was a strange experience. The room was completely silent. And it looked even bigger than it did before. I'd spent much of the past four days in this room, but as I stood in it now – stripped bare and quiet – it took on a whole new atmosphere. It seemed like a really calming space. On a stage at the opposite end of the room from the one we had watched Prince's friends and bandmates perform on, stood a number of his outfits. The *1999* trench coat was there, which made me laugh. Someone had obviously spotted the error I had noticed the day before – when the coat had been mistakenly displayed in the *Purple Rain* Room – and repositioned it. Next to the trench coat were Prince's black pinstripe suit, and the red shirt and hat he wore for the incredible 2004 Rock and Roll Hall of Fame performance of 'While My Guitar Gently Weeps'. Jonathan, Ben and I looked at the outfits up close and then walked across the Soundstage – away from the rest of our tour party – and we climbed up onto the hallowed stage, just for a second.

We moved on to the NPG Music Club, and while Mitch talked about Prince performing on the tiny stage, I took the opportunity to quietly walk to the back of the room. Standing beneath the front end of the Cadillac that is featured on the front of the *Sign o' the Times* album sleeve – I'd noticed it on our first day at the 'Prince Interactive' panel discussion – I lifted my arm up, and gently stroked the grille. Rejoining the group, we headed to the backstage area where the merchandise stall and entrance to the food marquee had been during *Celebration 2017*.

Mitch concluded the tour here, and he spoke briefly about Prince and what he had meant to him personally. I'd gathered – from his enthusiasm and knowledge – during the tour that he was a big *fam*, and my hunch had proved correct. Mitch told us how he felt working at Paisley Park was a privilege and coming to work in Prince's home every day was like a dream come true. He ended by inviting us to watch Prince's phenomenal 2007 Super Bowl XLI half-time show from Miami. We stood and watched the ten minute performance, and he thanked us for coming. As the tour ended, most of the attendees made their way outside. The merchandise stall was open and we spotted some beautiful posters that hadn't been on sale at *Celebration 2017*, so I picked some up. At the side of the stall was a notice offering a choice of dishes prepared by Prince's personal chef.

The opportunity to eat a last meal in Prince's house before

leaving was too good to miss, so we ordered food and I sat in the deserted marquee while Jonathan and Ben freshened up. There was just me and a woman eating her lunch, and I asked if her food was good. She nodded and smiled, and I asked her where she had travelled from. She said that she was from New York. We spoke for a minute or two before my companions returned and our food arrived a few minutes later. It felt strange to be inside Prince's home with virtually no one around – at least in this part of the building anyway. I'd ordered a grilled cheese sandwich with Gouda and Cheddar. It had slices of apple and honey pressed into it. It smelled amazing and tasted just as good.

After we'd eaten, we decided it was finally time to go. Stepping outside we took some photos of the building close-up, and headed through the complex to the parking lot out front. As we reached it – to my surprise – we spotted Mark. He was just arriving at the complex for a tour. He looked across to us and smiled, giving us a thumbs-up. We waved to each other and he disappeared inside. As of writing, it was the last time we saw each other. We're hoping to rectify that soon. Before we left, I quickly walked over to Paisley Park and placed my hands and face against the wall. It didn't feel cold. We stopped again outside the gate to take a last look at the sign, and I grabbed some photos of the little purple padlocks – containing lyrics from some of his songs – that *fam* had left attached to the perimeter fence of Paisley Park a year before.

"Let's go," I finally said, and we walked up Audubon Road for the last time.

A little while later, we arrived at Minneapolis-Saint Paul Airport and I drove to the car rental parking lot. I handed over the keys and we followed the signs for US Customs. After going through the security scanner – and while waiting for my bag in the x-ray machine – a female security officer called me over to her and performed a quick body search on me, and as she did so she asked me why I had been in Minneapolis. I told her about my journey, and we chatted for a minute before she said I could go.

As I said thanks, she suddenly said, "Oh my God, you're awesome!"

It took me by surprise. I smiled and replied, "So are you," and her cheeks flushed with colour.

As I walked away, Jonathan – who was behind me in the queue – glanced at her sideways and then said to me, "Did she just say you were awesome?"

I smiled and said that she had.

"Well, that's not very professional, is it?" he said – totally deadpan – and we laughed and headed for our gate.

EPILOGUE

I never imagined that many people would be interested in my experience in Minneapolis. Like I said at the beginning of this book, I undertook the journey for me. I'm not an important person. That's why this book isn't really about me. I'm just one of millions of others who love a particular artist – and like anyone else who isn't famous – the only people who are really interested in my life are my family and friends. I knew the few friends I had who were Prince *fam* would want to know everything that had happened, but the response I got when I arrived home took me completely by surprise. I have to say that I also never intended to write an account of the trip. My wife *did* suggest that I make some notes about the things I saw – particularly the Paisley Park events as we were not allowed to take photographs – and I'd mentioned to Jonathan on our last day that I was going to make some notes, but it was more as a record for my own enjoyment, perhaps a half-dozen pages that I could pull out of a drawer and read from time to time to remind myself that it had all actually happened.

Upon my return to the UK, it quickly became apparent to me that the journey I had been on was becoming something else altogether, a life-changing event which would ultimately culminate in me writing this book. To be honest, I've written it as much for my own memory – and Jonathan, Ben and Mark's – as anything else. It sounds silly, but I feel that the pilgrimage I made – and my boundless enthusiasm about it – perhaps makes people who know me feel good in some little way, in the same way it makes me feel good. I really do have some great friends. I think the fact I didn't intentionally set out to produce this book appeals to people too. Everything that has occurred since I got back, from conversing with members of Prince's bands – yes, *really* – to writing these words, has come about largely by happy accident.

To be honest – and this will no doubt make my friends laugh – I don't enjoy being the centre of attention and I'm not particularly good at speaking in public. In fact, the thought of standing in front of people and talking about myself fills me with dread, but since returning from Prince's hometown I have found myself doing just that. The audiences I've spoken to – Prince is my favourite subject to talk about, of course – seem to appreciate my account and have liked the photographs I have shown them, and I can truthfully say that I've enjoyed the experience very much. Speaking about Prince more – particularly since my trip – has led to people I'm acquainted with who weren't that familiar with his work investigating him further. Subsequently, I now have a lot more friends who enjoy Prince's music which – for me – is justification for all of the years I spent as a solitary Prince obsessive trying to share his wonderful music. It's made me feel like I was right about the little guy all along, which is really great. Everybody likes to be right now and then, don't they?

As for me and Prince, my love and respect for him has grown immeasurably since Minneapolis. I feel much closer to him as a person than I did before. Visiting his childhood homes has unquestionably made him more 'real' to me now. He is no longer the impenetrable rock star on a stage or screen that he once was. He is a real person. The pilgrimage I made is something I will never ever forget. Aside from family stuff, it's one of the greatest things I've done, and perhaps ever will do. Prince has been such a huge part of my life – and for so long – that it's difficult to think of anything I may do in the future that will be as important to me. The reception I received from everyone on my experience was amazing, and it's a testament to the wonderful people of the

Twin Cities that Prince never felt the urge to leave and make his home elsewhere. If he had, I doubt the journey would have had the same emotional resonance with me.

When I think back to the places I saw and people I met, I feel immensely proud of Prince. He wasn't groomed for stardom from childhood like some performers are. From inauspicious beginnings he rose up to become one of the greats. To reach the level of fame that Prince did takes some doing. Through a combination of incredible ability, fierce determination, and a work ethic second-to-none, he managed to achieve what most people can only dream about. He shared his gift too, helping other artists whenever and wherever he could. For that I feel he has to be applauded.

The journey I made was important to me from a healing perspective, and I'd hoped that it would make his passing hurt a little less. I genuinely believe that it has done so. For the majority of the time I was in Minnesota, I wasn't upset or melancholy. I'd been joyful. And I have felt like that since returning home too. I am immensely grateful to Prince for that. From learning a little more about his life, I have found myself thinking less about his death and more about what he has meant to me and how he has impacted on my life.

I'm also eternally grateful to him for the countless shows that I was fortunate to attend throughout the years. As an entertainer, I truly believe we will never see the likes of Prince again. In live performance his calibre was unmatched, and he will be sorely missed by anyone who ever witnessed him onstage. For me, he remains simply the greatest musician of an age.

Perhaps inevitably, I've listened to nothing but his music since April. And what incredible music it is. I'm sure it will play on for decades, and I hope – no, I *know* – that there are Prince *fam* who haven't been born yet who will love his music just as much as I and his millions of followers do. Ultimately, that is the legacy that Prince leaves behind, a body of work that will be loved by generations to come. And it is a legacy that any great creative mind surely strives for during their lifetime. For this skinny kid from Minneapolis – who came from nothing, seized every opportunity, danced his ass off, and ultimately conquered the world – it had been paramount. He really was one of 'The Beautiful Ones'.

♥

POSTSCRIPT

It's two o'clock in the morning and I just can't sleep. We moved house a month ago and, to be honest, I'm having trouble adjusting to a different place. It's the last week of July 2018 and we're in the middle of a two month heatwave. That may be a factor too. I recall someone saying that it hasn't rained properly since May 24th. I look away from the ceiling, where my gaze has been directed for several minutes, and glance across to my phone. It flashes intermittently with notifications. I rise and cross the room. I have several messages. I open the first. I don't recognise the sender's name, but I have a feeling I'll know what it says. It begins like this, "Hello Stuart. I hope you don't mind me contacting you, but I've just read your book." I smile and read the rest of the message that has been sent across the globe in an instant. It's a scenario that happens more than you would think, and, more often than not, this contact comes from people who are not in the same country as me, or even the same continent. Sometimes I receive several messages a week. It's been pretty constant since my book came out in November last year. A lot come from the US, but I've heard from people as far away from me as Australia too. Every time I open one of these messages, it reminds me just how far my incredible experience on the first anniversary of Prince's passing has travelled and what the pilgrimage has become to others. And to me. Many people have told me they've travelled to Minneapolis and used my book as a guide.

Others impart that they are planning a trip there, and that Minneapolis Reign has been the catalyst that provided the initiative to do so. Whenever I hear this, I feel immensely proud that I have been able to help fellow Prince fans fulfil their ambition to learn more about where our musical hero grew up and how he developed his immeasurable talent as a musician and performer.

When the book launched in late 2017, I had no idea who would buy it, or whether people would like it. Looking back now, it was perhaps naive of me, but I genuinely thought that nobody would be interested in it. My instinct proved incorrect almost from the get go. I'll come to that shortly.

I arrived back from Minneapolis in the last week of April 2016. Before I knew it, it was June and summer was here. I found myself in the somewhat surreal surroundings of an office at the BBC, waiting to go on the radio to talk about what I'd seen in Prince's hometown. Thinking about it now, I can't even recall how that situation came about. I'm pretty sure that it was the first time I'd told anyone about the book I was planning to write though. In fact, the name of the book hadn't even been finalised and I think I said it incorrectly on air. Nonetheless, it was now out there. I was committed to writing a book about Prince. There was no going back, and the thought of putting pen to paper – or fingers to keys, as it were – absolutely terrified me. It also made me realise my next problem. I didn't actually own a computer.

Fortunately a friend, Nick, came to the rescue and gifted me a laptop. A brand new computer. I was overwhelmed. It was an unbelievably generous gesture. I set to work and the next four months became a blur of late nights, bleary eyes and tea. Lots of tea. I spent hours poring over maps to meticulously retrace my steps and double-check the order of the carefully planned itinerary I had followed in Minneapolis. My wife kept the kids out of the way, and the piles of paper on our dining room table grew and grew. Finally, after weeks of writing, rewriting, and asking my wife's opinion, I finished the first book I'd ever written. I carefully read through Minneapolis Reign a dozen times from beginning to end, before calling my publisher to tell them I was done.

I nervously sent across the first draft and awaited a response to my work. I didn't have to wait long. Graeme called me a few days later and told me that he'd read my manuscript. I asked him what he thought of it. "It's amazing", he replied. "I love it." I was over the moon. We agreed a date of November 10th 2017 for the book's release and the official website presale began shortly after that. I also organised a launch party at The Georgian Theatre, a historic local venue in the cultural quarter of my town. A few weeks later I received proof copies of Minneapolis Reign. It was incredible to see the words I'd typed just a few weeks earlier on the page. The book looked sensational. I couldn't believe it had my name on it. I had several meetings with Graeme, and he made sure I was happy with the finished book before it went to print.

It took what felt like an eternity for the release date to come around. In reality, it was only about six weeks. The launch party took place a few days before the official publication date, and the venue was packed. Initial copies of Minneapolis Reign were available on the night, and I signed dozens of books for people and posed for photos with lots of friends and family. My parents, who live in Western Asia, were in the UK. They attended and told everyone how proud they were. I actually spotted people reading my book at tables too. I was overwhelmed at the comments the book had, and couldn't believe that so many people had come. It was an amazing evening. At the same time, online orders started to come in quickly and this was the first inkling I had that Minneapolis Reign might become something much bigger than I'd anticipated.

In the run-up to all of this, Prince's Estate had announced an exhibition at the former Millennium Dome in London, now known as the O2. It was to feature Prince's personal effects and many of his instruments. It had been exactly a decade since Prince's now legendary 2007 Earth Tour residency at the venue, which had taken place over twenty-one nights that summer. I had attended several incredible shows and after-show parties during his run there, and it had been an amazing time to be a Prince fan. Reviews at the time proclaimed him the greatest entertainer on the planet. I immediately booked a ticket for the My Name Is Prince Exhibition. It opened in late October. I chose to attend on the same day that the book was released: November 10th.

Copies of Minneapolis Reign were now being distributed to all corners of the globe, and I began receiving messages of support as well as many friend requests on social media. The book was now being printed worldwide and I was shocked at how it had taken off. Copies were sent to several people featured in it, including Morris Hayes – Prince's one-time Musical Director and keyboard player in the New Power Generation, Prince's former backing band. Morris had contacted me out of the blue after hearing about the book, offering his congratulations. I'd cheekily replied by asking if I could use his quote on the cover. He agreed. I felt this would add some cachet to the book. It looked great too.

On November 10th – launch day – I drove down to Greenwich in London, and the site of Prince's 2007 concerts. I parked in the same spot I had when I'd attended those shows a decade earlier. I was immediately taken right back there. I could even picture the huge billboards advertising the Earth Tour shows that were fixed to the lampposts around the building. I smiled as I remembered. I'd put ten copies of Minneapolis Reign in my bag, figuring I may see people from his inner circle, who I could give a free copy to. Unfortunately, I didn't get the opportunity to do so. In a bar inside the O2, I was greeted by several fellow fans I had met online. They asked if I had the book with me, and the copies I'd brought were gone within a minute. But I kept one back. It was great to meet everyone and we spent a few hours chatting before the exhibition began.

As I queued to enter, there was a palpable air of anticipation. I wondered if the things I'd seen in Prince's home would be there. I'd booked the VIP tour, and a group of twenty of us were taken into a room away from the main exhibition hall. Here, we saw items such as Prince's make-up kit and the instrument cases used at the shows in this very building ten years previous. A case contained dozens of pairs of his custom-made shoes and nearby a screen played a recording of one of the shows I had attended. The highlight of the tour then took place. We were seated in a small room, and there in the corner was Prince's custom purple Taylor 612 CE guitar. He had been the last person to play it and it had been used extensively during his Musicology Tour in 2004. We were told we were able to hold the guitar. This drew audible gasps. We took it in turns to hold and study the beautiful instrument. Everyone was incredibly careful with it. We then moved into the main exhibition space. It was filled with hundreds of artefacts from Prince's career. Handwritten lyrics and album sleeve drawings sat alongside awards and outfits that were well known to every Prince fam. At one point, I stood next to a shirt worn during the Sign o' the Times Tour in 1987, and I marvelled at how it had been coloured in using felt-tip pens. Lots of the stage outfits were incredibly delicate, and although each outfit was easily within touching distance – and not behind protective screens – I didn't see a single person do so. I felt it was a significant indicator of how precious we all thought these possessions of our shared musical hero were, not only to him, but to us too. We continued through the exhibition and toward the end a replica tribute fence – like the one at Paisley Park – had been erected for fam to leave their mementos and messages. A sign said that the items would be taken back to Minneapolis and preserved in the official archive. I placed the last remaining copy of Minneapolis Reign I had in my bag on the fence, right at the top, way out of reach. I left London and immediately booked another ticket. This time I chose the final day of the exhibition, a few days after New Year. I figured it would be the last time I'd ever see his things.

Christmas came and went, and the book sold steadily across the holiday season and into 2018. The record store I own a share in sold the book, and I had lots of people come in and ask me about the trip. I was invited to take part in several podcasts in the US and my work began to receive widespread recognition, often from people who were important in the Prince community. Alex Hahn and Laura Tiebert, who I'd met in Minneapolis and who were authors of definitive Prince books themselves, offered their support and championed Minneapolis Reign, even going so far as to review it online. Duane Tudahl, also a writer of an incredible Prince book, became a friend. We talked often about how things were going with our respective tomes. Another big moment came when Jason Draper, a renowned author – and a huge Prince fan – reviewed the book for Record Collector magazine. We corresponded for a while afterward and he was really great. He told me that he would use the book himself as a guide when he was next in Minnesota.

By now, I had become acquainted with several people connected directly to Prince throughout the years, and all of them were gracious, friendly and open to talking to me. Among them was Jeremiah Freed aka Dr Funkenberry. Jeremiah, a California-based blogger who runs an entertainment website, had developed a close personal friendship with Prince in 2012, and had become a kind of unofficial spokesman for him, often giving fam exclusive information regarding upcoming events at Paisley Park. Throughout what unexpectedly became the last few years of Prince's life, Jeremiah was regarded as an extremely important figure in the Prince community. In the weeks after Prince's passing, Jeremiah was in high demand for interviews on TV and radio, and he spoke warmly about the man he had come to regard as a friend. To hear from him was amazing. Jeremiah is a really nice guy. I had also made firm friends with lots of fans of his music, and we share stories and even send each other Prince stuff through the mail. I have received some incredible artwork from some of them. Everyone was really supportive of Minneapolis Reign too. It felt like I'd become a member of a huge extended worldwide family, and every member loved the same things I did, and were just as – and, in some cases, even more – obsessed with Prince as I was. Many told me they felt the same way about him that I did, and it felt good to be a part of something so great.

On January 7th, I travelled down to London for the final day of the My Name Is Prince Exhibition. In the main hall, I spoke to dozens of people, all of whom recognised me. For over four hours in that room I barely looked at anything. I spent the whole time in conversation with people who'd bought my book. I actually felt like a celebrity. It was totally surreal. I left London on a real high and a short while later I received a message to say my book had been safely transported to Paisley Park along with the other tributes from the fence and was now in the official Prince archive. I was over the moon.

As 2018 went on, I was invited to attend two Prince conventions. I say conventions. Parties would be a more accurate description. The first, in Edinburgh, was an opportunity to meet lots of the people I'd become friends with over the previous year for the first time. Everyone had a great night and the DJ played nothing but Prince all night. The second took place in Birmingham just a few months ago. Again, I met a number of people I had only previously talked to on social media. I also added a whole new bunch of friends to the ever-growing list of fellow Prince fam I'd become acquainted with.

By now, Minneapolis Reign was a bestseller. I couldn't believe the journey I had been on since April 2017. It sounds silly, but the best thing about everything that has happened to me is actually just a little thing. I often like to look at my cabinet of books about Prince. I pretty much have them all and I've read every single one of them. There amongst them is one written about an incredible journey with my hero. And it has my name on it. The thrill of seeing it is still indescribable.

THANK YOU

In (almost) no particular order, my eternal gratitude goes to:

Graeme Wilkinson. You have changed my life with this thing. Thanks, mate.

C.G. Hatton, Alex Hahn, Laura Tiebert, Jason Draper, Michael Byars, Amy L. Bolling, Phil Simms, Mark Bruton, Tami Neubaeur Foster, Bill Aitken, Andrew Johnson, Dan Briggs, Anth Knight, Ken Norris, Steve Johnson, Philip Clarkson, Joan Alythia, Phil Dunn, Mark Jennings, Andy Foot, Tony Smithyman, Andrew Povey, Susan Jefferson, Pascal Besselink, Gary Walters, Karen Surmiak, Nigel Hart, Dawn Cooper, Claudy Lubbers, Maisie Hall, Carolyn Chester, Chris Bailey, Martyn Levitt, Michael Sargent, Hamish Whitta, Morris Hayes, Shelby Johnson, Monica McKnight, Jeannine Gila, Christian Tyler, Ann-Marie Smith, Henrietta Lyttelton, Si Evans, Katie Jones, Duane Tudahl, Jacqueline Smith, Chris Dibb-Fuller, Pedro Baird, Joanne Vaughan, Craig McMahon, Jamie Donnelly, Craig Wood, Pippa Fellowes, Kevin Gallagher, Dale Gothfather, Greg Robinson, Jordan Bell, Simon Hall, Mark Rogers, Kelly Laybourne, the Sound it Out Records crew, Leigh Morton, Jamie Halliday, Stephen Gill, Gurk Nainu, Alan Formby-Jackson, Dan Donnelly, Susana Cervantes, Rich Short, Carolyn Williams, Dave Murray, Elle Richardson, Bart Hermans, James Taylor, Graeme Hoey, June Patrice Daly, Enza Rosa, Anthony Bachelor, Louisa Garbutt, Richard Thornton, Jill

Fullick, Mark Fullick, Debbie Coppinger, Ricci Terranova, Pook Berry, Adele Burchi, John Kirkbride, Aid Cooper, Kim Somers Egelsee, Amy Marrero, Zach Hoskins, Andrea Tait, Donna Day Triplett, Johnny Sands, Julie Waines, Andrew Boyle, Alison Howells DiMascio, Susan Quinn, Emma Raines, Emma Newman, Jes Jeffery, Alison McKenzie, Angela Canova, Pilar Rick, Karen Morrissey, Danny Cooper, Anita Desai, James Edge, Laura Ann Hind, Becky Barron, Ben Muriel, Mark Fitzpatrick, Kingsley Hall, David Saunders, Lydia Gooding, Alex Foster, Erica Daniels, F.A. Robinson, Bethan Blake, Alan Bradley, Mark Spindles Allen, Mark Werrett, Martien Dergent, Billy Hodson, Debbie Poli, Bob Fischer, Lee Hall, Lisa Ingham, Marty Yule, Maryann Emilio, Stephanie Cullen, Maureen O'Sullivan, Maxine Martin, Alan Bradley, Alan Kagan, Darren Thomas, Martin Hutchinson, Martin Whitell, Sue Whitell, Alison Hilton, Buse Unver, Helen Pedder, Gabrielle Sidaway, Sharon McAllister, Carl Green, Graeme Braby, Cath Walsh, Janice Weinstein Waterman, Stephen Peter McLean, Michael O'Reilly, Micky York, Mike Russell, Molly Chard, Catherine Gallagher, Janine Crawford, John Paul McQue, Catherine McLean, Renata Lehmann, Rich Whitfield, Richard Vernon, Ian Dixon, Rupert Lewis, Ruth Beavis, Sam Weatherley, Cecile van Ooij, Chi Chi Wagmann, Dixie Reetz, Chloe Gourlay, Ste Allen, Jeanette Norton, Nick Wesson, Nicole Walton, Paul Harvey, Phil Elener, Stu Blackburn, Stuart Armstrong, Vincent Hugh Lacey, Trevor Haggan, Wendy Gibson Carroll, Ian Boddy, Will Nett, Pippa Roberts, Marco t'Hart, Christine Donfrancesco, Ian Luck, Ian Wallace, Simon Howard Briggs, James Barker, Ludivina Nieto, Christopher Arnel, David Pearson, Chris Cobain, Kylie Cobain, Rachel Branson, Sophie Gatehouse, Timothy Oxnard, Neil Perryman, Sue Perryman, Nicol Perryman, Neil Woodyatt, Stuie Powell, Dunstan Bruce, Howard M. Bedford, Helen Wells, Scott Wetherill, Shane Healey, Sheryl Watson, Mark Watson, Claire Dupree, Mark Whiteside, Claire Flanders, Clare M. Rountree, Coleen Shaw-Voeks, James Watson, Patty Sullivan, The Purple Army, NPGUK, all of the Prince alumni I have had the pleasure to talk to, my parents Lawrence and Georgina, my children, and last but by no means least my amazing wife, Paula. I know I thank her in the acknowledgements at the beginning of this book but her input and support cannot be underestimated. She is the driving force behind all that I am and I owe all of this to her. Her faith in me is unwavering at all times and she is simply the greatest human being I have ever known. If you're reading this, Mrs Willoughby, I love you alleweld.

It's taken me a while to compile this list. If I've forgotten anyone, I offer my sincerest apologies. The last year has definitely been the weirdest of my life. Thank you for buying my book. It means so much to me. I hope it does to you too.

Stu x

PRINCE IN PRINT

Azhar, Mobeen. 2017. *Prince: Stories From The Purple Underground.* Carlton.

Draper, Jason. 2011. *Prince: Chaos, Disorder, and Revolution.* Backbeat.

Draper, Jason. 2017. *Prince, Life & Times.* Chartwell.

Garcia, Mayte. 2017. *The Most Beautiful: My Life With Prince.* Trapeze.

Greenman, Ben. 2017. *Dig If You Will The Picture, Funk, Sex and God in the Music of Prince.* Faber & Faber.

Hahn, Alex. 2003. *Possessed, The Rise and Fall of Prince.* Billboard Books.

Hahn, Alex and Tiebert, Laura. 2017. *The Rise of Prince 1958 -1988.* Mad Cat Press.

Hill, Dave. 1989. *Prince: A Pop Life.* Faber & Faber.

Hoskins, Barney. 1988. *Prince: Imp of the Perverse.* Virgin.

Jones, Liz. 1998. *Purple Reign, The Artist Formerly Known As Prince.* Birch Lane Press.

Light, Alan. 2014. *Let's Go Crazy, Prince and the Making of Purple Rain.* Atria.

Morton, Brian. 2007. *Prince, A Thief In The Temple.* Canongate.

Nilsen, Per. 1999. *Prince: The First Decade – Dancemusicsexromance.* Firefly.

Nilsen, Per and Mattheij, Joozt. 2004. *The Vault, The Definitive Guide to the Musical World of Prince.* Uptown.

Ro, Ronin. 2012. *Prince: Inside The Music and the Masks.* Aurum

Thorne, Matt. 2012. *Prince.* Faber & Faber.

Touré. 2013. *I Would Die 4 U: Why Prince Became An Icon.* Atria.

Walsh, Jim. 2017. *Gold Experience, Following Prince in the '90s.* University of Minnesota Press.

PRINCE ONLINE

officialprincemusic.com

officialpaisleypark.com

princevault.com

princeonlinemuseum.com

prince.org

Printed by Amazon Italia Logistica S.r.l.
Torrazza Piemonte (TO), Italy

1180011/R00132